HARD CROCHET

HARD CROCHET

Mark Dittrick

HAWTHORN BOOKS, INC.
PUBLISHERS/NEW YORK
A Howard & Wyndham Company

FOR DIANE

Photographs by Lloyd Freidus unless otherwise credited.

Photograph appearing on page 6 is copyright ©1977 Downe Publishing, Inc. Reprinted with permission of *Ladies' Home Journal Needle & Craft*.

HARD CROCHET

Library of Congress Catalog Card Number: 76–56512

ISBN: 0–8015–3279–5 Hardbound edition
ISBN: 0–8015–3280–9 Paperbound edition
    4 5 6 7 8 9 10

Contents

HARD CROCHET

HARD CROCHET: WHAT IT IS AND WHAT IT ISN'T

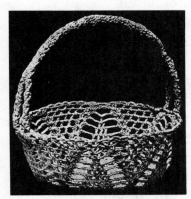

The following instructions appeared in the August 1927 issue of *Needlecraft* magazine:

There are several methods of treating these baskets; that which I generally use and find satisfactory is as follows: Dissolve one cupful of sugar in a half cupful of water and boil until it "spins a thread" or strings when poured from the spoon. Have the basket thoroughly moistened, so it will absorb the syrup evenly, and use the latter as you would starch, putting the basket into it and rubbing the syrup into the work until all parts are covered. The basket should not be wet—wring or squeeze as dry as possible after saturating it; simply have it evenly dampened. After it has been stiffened with the syrup, stretch it over a mold of the right size and shape—a three quart kettle was used for the basket illustrated—and put in a warm oven, or over the stove on a rack to harden. Be sure the handle keeps its shape, rounding it as it begins to dry. When thoroughly dry it is ready for use. If a coat of shellac, and one or two coats of varnish are applied, after stiffening, letting each coat become perfectly dry before applying the next, the basket will hold its shape indefinitely, and may be wiped off with a damp cloth. If this treatment is not given, the basket must, of course, be again stiffened and molded should it be necessary to wash or cleanse it.

Hard crochet is a new technique for making crochet that is rigid. The basket shown on the previous page is crocheted; it is also rigid; but it's not Hard Crochet. Made over fifty years ago, this basket, along with its not so subtle stiffening instructions, is reproduced here to show that the concept of making something that's both crocheted and rigid is not a particularly new one. It also serves to demonstrate that all rigid crochet is not Hard Crochet.

Crocheting rigidly did not end with the candy-coated basket. In fact, the idea has come quite a long way since 1927. In recent years, many innovative crocheters have experimented with new methods and a wide range of unusual materials—twines, cords, raffia, plastics, leather, and even wire—to produce stiff, stand-on-their-own objects and forms. The usually successful fruits of such experiments were works often as beautiful as they were unique. The few examples reproduced on these pages amply testify to that fact.

All of these recent rigid crochet techniques have something in common, a thing that separates them from the fifty-year-old basket: They all depend on and exploit the natural rigidness of the material crocheted; this is where the rigidness comes from, not from any after-the-crocheting-is-done stiffening process—the more rigid the material crocheted, the more rigid the resulting crochet.

These rigid techniques have something else in common, something they even have in common with that shellac-covered basket: None of them is Hard Crochet.

Hard Crochet is fundamentally different from any other rigid-crochet technique. I can best explain what that difference is in a rather roundabout way, beginning at the beginning, back in the summer of 1970 when I did what seemed in those preliberation times like a pretty courageous thing for a big, strong, red-blooded American boy to do—I learned to crochet.

Like most crocheters just starting out (regardless of gender) I began by doing everything wrong that could be done wrong, including making all my stitches much too tight. Most novice crocheters, if they have any talent at all for the craft, soon overcome this obviously negative

Fairly thick twine and a large, strong hook were used by Barbara Muccio to craft this beautifully rigid basket.

Another classic basket by Barbara Muccio, this time crocheted with plastic-coated wire.

Del Feldman crocheted spiraling rounds around a spiraling rope armature to make these handsome baskets so stiff and rigid.

habit; they learn to control the tension on their yarn and begin making nice, loose, peekaboo stitches. For me, though, conquering the beginner's-tendency-to-crochet-too-tight syndrome was a whole lot more easily said than done.

"Loosen up!" I was admonished, time and time again. "Crochet is supposed to be flexible—F L E X I B L E !"

"That's what you think; I'll show you," I'd like to say that I said in reply. But I didn't. And pretty soon, I was churning out nice, acceptable, flimsy, see-through crochet, just like everyone else.

To create the more rigid components of her beautifully sculptural body ornaments, Ruth Nivola crochets very thin metallic yarn into tight tubes which are then beaten flat and stiff.

As a male and a crocheter, I was confronted with what must be a fairly common problem among male crocheters; I had a lot of trouble deciding what to crochet. I had absolutely no need (I'll swear to this on Bibles) and even less desire to make such time-honored and traditional crochetables as granny-square halter tops, frilly, filet-stitched shawls, or heirloom bedspreads. Having scarved myself half to death during the winter of 1970, I was forced to search for more useful and, I have to confess, more macho things to crochet.

Before long, I came across a particularly good-looking Stetson-type western hat. It had a beautiful, deep-dented crown and a handsome, wide, gracefully upturning brim. It was exactly the sort of thing I'd been looking for, and I decided that there was no reason why I shouldn't be able to reproduce it in crochet.

I quickly had the making of the hat all figured out—the shaping, the increasing, everything. Knowing that no ordinary crochet yarn could give me the texture or firmness needed, I took some beautiful, thick wool yarn I'd obtained from a weaver and began crocheting. Soon, the fruits of my labor lay before me (and *lay* is the word for it): a soggy-crowned, floppy-brimmed, very un-Stetson-like hat that left macho to be desired.

What went wrong? I wondered. Then it dawned on me: I had actually crocheted something too loosely—not too tight, but too loose. I was overjoyed. I rapidly ripped out the whole mess of mushy stitches. (*Ripping out* in crochet is a way of undoing something that's been done incorrectly so that it can be redone correctly, a technique I would find very useful in life.) and started crocheting the hat all over again, this time more tightly than before and with a smaller crochet hook. The second hat was still too flimsy. I ripped out again and made the hat over, much tighter than the previous two and using a still smaller hook. Pretty soon, as I recall, the crown on that hat started getting stiffer and stiffer, and the same thing happened to the brim. And the tighter I crocheted, the stiffer it got. I crocheted that hat as tight as I could; I wanted it to be as stiff as I could possibly make it. Not flexible, but stiff, S T I F F !

Unlike other forms of rigid crochet, what stiffness had been achieved was due to the tightness of the stitches, not to the rigidness of the yarn. And I figured that this was as stiff as yarn could be crocheted.

"So that's Hard Crochet," you might be saying to yourself. If so, you would only be partly right. Yes, it was the first important step in the evolution of what was to become Hard Crochet, but a very necessary ingredient was still missing. Allow me to continue.

I became, in time, a very good crocheter—the result, I'm sure, of some well-disposed genes. So proficient had I become, in fact, that before very long I was coauthoring (with Susan Morrow) a book on the craft entitled *Contemporary Crochet*. When it appeared, the book had one of

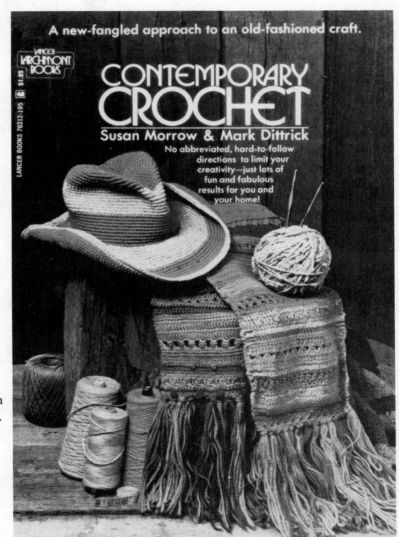

Very early Hard Crochet: the hat on the cover of *Contemporary Crochet*.

Tighter-than-normal projects from the pages of *Contemporary Crochet*.

the Stetson-type hats right on the cover, and inside, along with some very nice scarves, traditionally crocheted hats, vests, and the like, were a few tighter-than-normal-crochet projects crocheted from such materials as cotton, wool, twine, and flax—hints of the yet-to-be-fully-developed Hard Crochet.

The book's Appendix contained a list of yarn suppliers. In preparing it, yarn samples were sent for from every entry under "Yarn" in the legendary *Whole Earth Catalog*. They soon began pouring in, everything from bulky hand-spun and hand-dyed wool yarns to shocking pink macramé cord. One group of yarns was most interesting; this is how the Appendix listing for the supplier appeared:

THE MANNINGS CREATIVE CRAFTS
R.D. 2
East Berlin, Pennsylvania 17316

Some of the most unusual yarns we've seen. Hard, weaving-type yarns in various weights, some of which have several colors in them twisted around each other. Reasonable prices; samples FREE.

The samples of this yarn had not been sent away for until the book was almost finished; consequently, none of the yarn was used for any of the things in the book. In fact, it wasn't until quite some time after the book was completed that I finally got around to ordering a quantity of the yarn to try.

Accustomed to buying yarn by the skein and twines and cords in balls, I was unprepared for the way the yarns from The Mannings arrived—foot-high cones wrapped fat with yarn. This was my first experience with buying *mill ends*, the tail-end leavings and discontinued lots of yarn from high-volume mills and factories. I was very impressed.

For a while I crocheted fairly loosely with the yarns from The Mannings, unaware that the way they came on

A large cone of three-ply carpet yarn.

Multicolored & Synthetic Yarn

$2.50 PER LB

$2.65 PER LB. WEST OF THE MISSISSIP

approx. 5

MINIMUM ORDE

A bundle of yarn samples from The Mannings.

cones wasn't the only unusual thing about them. Then I decided to try a hat, like the one on the cover of *Contemporary Crochet.* I worked the way I had for the wool hat, crocheting as tightly as I possibly could. The results were nothing short of amazing—the hat came out at least twice as stiff and rigid as the hat on the cover. "This is some kind of yarn!" I thought to myself, "And it isn't nearly as thick as the wool I used for the other hat. What is it?" I looked at the samples I had ordered the yarn from and found the answer.

Is there any way to whisper something on a printed page, so as not to shock the reader? I guess not, so I'll just have to come out with it: The yarns from The Mannings, the yarns that worked up in such an incredibly rigid way, were (a long, nervous pause) *synthetic.*

Why all the apprehension? Because it's an undeniable fact that some people (especially ultracraftsy types) will have nothing to do with anything that isn't one hundred and twenty-five percent natural. For them, the term *synthetic* ranks right up there with *red dye #2* and *oil spill.* And I guess it's a feeling that's only natural (no play on the word intended) in this no-preservative, no-additive age of Granola, spray can bans, and organic gardening— all of them things near and dear to me.

However, I happen to find nothing wrong with synthetic yarns. They are, in my only slightly biased opinion, the unfortunate victims of the current tide of ecological concern. Indeed, speaking of unfortunate victims, think for a moment how many beautiful and defenseless animals would be spared if all fur were synthetic. I rest my case.

The yarns I'm talking about are rug yarns, *real* rug yarns—the kind of yarn used in the manufacture of wall-to-wall carpeting—not the yarns that pass for rug yarns in your local five-and-dime. That yarn would turn off a robot. In fact, these yarns are so different from the dime-store variety that I began referring to them as carpet yarns to avoid confusion.

I was soon crocheting exclusively with the new yarn. And for quite a long while I made only hats with it, con-

Lloyd Freidus (in a characteristically serious pose) wearing an early rigid hat crocheted with natural flax cord. PHOTO BY THE AUTHOR.

Another view. Lloyd's hat remained very rigid . . . until he wore it out in the rain. PHOTO BY THE AUTHOR.

centrating on perfecting their construction and design. I made dozens of hats, selling them as quickly as I made them.

An occasional buyer would ask if he could wear his new hat out in the rain. I would nervously caution against it, recalling an unhappy experience I'd had shortly after the first wool hat had been made. I had crocheted a hat, a beautiful, rigid hat—like a rock it was—out of a very hard and rigid natural fiber called cable-laid flax. Lloyd Freidus, movie cameraman, photographer, and close

Aside from getting it clean, two washings in very hot water and harsh detergent had no effect on this, the author's **personal hat.** PHOTO BY BRUCE MEISLER.

friend, took one look at that hat and made me an unrefusable offer for it. Lloyd loved his new hat and wore it everywhere—on location, to the store, around the house, and, regrettably, out in the rain. That trip out in the rain took all the rigid out of the hat. The brim became so floppy that Lloyd had trouble seeing through the lens of his camera. You see, true-blue Lloyd kept right on wearing that hat—I think he was afraid my feelings would be hurt if he didn't. A month or two later, though, Lloyd lost the hat. I'm glad he did. I think Lloyd was happy, too.

As a result of the experience with Lloyd and his hat, I quite naturally assumed that the same thing—death by wetness—might happen to hats made with the new yarn; I had no reason to think anything else. And I held on to that assumption until the day I decided that my own personal hat (made with the carpet yarn) had gotten so dirty from constant wearing that I would have to either retire it or try somehow to clean it. I opted for the latter. Why not find out for sure what would happen to that hat, or anything else crocheted with the new yarn, if it got wet? So, I decided to test the hat in a really big way.

Using the harshest detergent I could find—I looked around for something with a name like Search and Destroy and had to settle for Bold—in a sink filled with painfully hot water, I laundered the daylights out of the hat. I worked back and forth over the surface of the crochet with a plastic-bristled scrub brush, getting out dirt accumulated during months of wear. The hat got very clean, but the important question was, What had happened to its rigidness? It took surprisingly little time for the hat to dry, and when it was removed from its clothespin, the question was answered: The washing had had no effect on the crochet; it was as rigid as ever. Elated, I continued to experiment with what I was beginning to think of as wonder yarn, unaware that it still held one more great surprise in store for me.

Everything crocheted with the new yarn up till then had been worked *in the round,* in spiraling rounds of stitches; so, I tried crocheting rigidly with them the other way, in back-and-forth rows. The crochet that resulted was not quite as rigid, and while the in-the-round crochet had virtually no elasticity, the back-and-forth work still had a little—not much, but some. Undaunted by the unspectacular outcome of this experiment and still inspired by my success in the soapy sink, I did something that seemed a little irrational at the time: Using a hot iron and lots of steam, I vigorously blocked a sample of the fairly rigid back-and-forth crochet. When I removed the iron, lifted away the towel, and picked up the still-steaming swatch, my first impression was that I had absolutely destroyed it; it was paper thin and had as much body as two-week-old lettuce. But as the swatch cooled, something quite miraculous began to happen: Its body and thickness gradually returned; then some of its rigidness came back. But something was missing: the elasticity. The swatch had become like a piece of leather—it had a leatherlike toughness and amazing strength. Here, I realized, was an entirely new side to this new craft technique, the technique I was finally ready to call Hard Crochet.

Two Kinds of Hard Crochet

Crochet stitches can be worked two different ways: (1) in back-and-forth rows and (2) in spiraling rounds. There are also two kinds of Hard Crochet—one worked in the round and the other back and forth.

Of the two kinds of Hard Crochet, the one worked in the round is the more rigid; crochet stitches worked very tightly in the round naturally produce a more rigid "fabric" than stitches worked just as tightly back and forth. Why? Beyond the obvious difference between the two ways of working—the flatness of one and the three-dimensionality of the other—there is a more subtle dissimilarity that may account for much of in-the-round Hard Crochet's superior rigidness. Spiraling rounds of stitches are worked in only one direction; consequently, each new stitch is made into the "front" of a stitch in the round below. Crochet worked back and forth, on the other hand, requires that the work be turned at the end of each completed row of stitches so that a new row of stitches can be worked over the previous one. As a result of this turning of the work, new stitches are worked into the "backs" of stitches in the previous row. But what does this have to do with rigidness? New stitches just seem to "lock into" other stitches more neatly and more tightly when worked into them from the front. This superior locking of stitches appears to be a major reason for the greater rigidity of Hard Crochet worked in the round.

Does the three-dimensionality of in-the-round Hard Crochet contribute to its rigidness? I suspect that it does play some small part. I once took a sample of very tightly worked back-and-forth crochet and, stitching its sides together, made a tube out of it just to see what effect, if any, the tube shape would have on the rigidness of the material. It had very little.

In-the-round Hard Crochet is extremely strong. Basket-like objects made with the technique can support a surprising amount of weight and have no difficulty maintaining their shapes. The hats on pages 132 and 136 and the baskets on pages 96, 101, 105, and 109 are all examples of Hard Crochet worked in the round.

In an impressive no-tricks display of weight-lifting ability, a tightly crocheted basket easily supports 22 pounds plus.

Though less rigid than Hard Crochet worked in the round, back-and-forth Hard Crochet that has been "superblocked" has its own unique kind of strength. When a veteran crocheter friend, a woman very wise in the ways of textiles, inspected a sample of the vigorously ironed and steamed material, she offered the opinion that it might have become felted. She explained how wool fibers, when subjected to pressure and moisture, mat together to form the tough, inelastic fabric we know as felt. This is indeed not unlike what happens to the synthetic yarn used for Hard Crochet when it experiences a very similar treatment. For want of a better explanation, I accepted my textile-wise, veteran crocheter friend's interpretation and began calling back-and-forth, super-blocked crochet "felted" Hard Crochet.

Back-and-forth crocheted material that is to be super-blocked does not have to be as tightly made as the in-the-round kind, making this type of work somewhat easier to execute for the beginning Hard Crocheter. After blocking, the back-and-forth crochet is very strong, inelastic, and leatherlike, qualities that suggest some of the uses to which felted Hard Crochet can be put. The attaché case on page 141 is a good example of this kind of Hard Crochet.

More About Yarns that Crochet Up Hard

Why do the yarns used for Hard Crochet behave the way they do? The sample tag had told me only that these were synthetic yarns, not what kind of synthetic yarn. I discovered that each of the cones on which the yarn was wound had a curious, cryptic label hidden inside. Two or three of the labels revealed lot numbers, surrounded by lots of other incomprehensible numbers. But the majority of the labels clearly stated that their yarn was "70 ACRYLIC, 30 MODACRYLIC." This was a beginning.

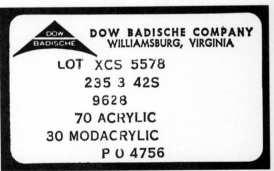

The label from a cone of carpet yarn reveals its fiber content: 70 percent acrylic, 30 percent modacrylic.

The word *acrylic* was far from unfamiliar, but I knew little more about it than that it referred to a material used in some paints, in a spray I've often used in drawing (Crystal Clear), and in various other things. (Who will ever forget the hammer-wielding housewife banging away at a slab of clear acrylic in that often-aired floor wax commercial?) *Modacrylic* was a total mystery to me. I headed for the library.

There I found a 928-page tome entitled *Man-Made Fibres* by R. W. Moncrieff. After glancing through the "Differences between Condensation and Addition Polymerisations," "Anistropic Swelling," "Surface Saponification," and "Stereospecific Catalysts," I finally found some passages better suited to my level of sophistication. I found out, for instance, that "there are many acrylic fibres: Orlon, Acrilan, Courtelle, Caslan are typical. There are only four modacrylic fibres: Verel, Dynel, Kanekalon and Teklan."

The field of only four fibers, the modacrylics, seemed to be the best place to start, so I looked up the fibers mentioned in the book's Index. The coverage of Verel was very sparse, but an entire chapter was devoted to Dynel. I found out that "there is little or no risk of fire with Dynel."

"One never knows when a fireproof hat might come in handy," I thought. I continued to read. "Dynel fabric buried in soil in tropical conditions was unchanged after six months, whereas a heavy cotton duck disintegrated after ten days."

While I couldn't help feeling sorry for the duck, this new revelation set me to thinking about what a wonderful potential Hard Crochet might have in the land of palm trees and coconuts. But the next passage I read made me quickly forget the tropics and fireproof hats. Under the heading "Resistance to Ironing," I learned that "Dynel is susceptible to *stiffening* [my italics] and shrinking if an ordinary hot iron set at the 'rayon' temperature is used. It has to be ironed with the lowest iron setting and a *dry* [my italics again] cotton cover with the fabric. This is a marked defect. . . ."

"Marked defect, my foot," I thought to myself. Could this be the explanation of what happened to felted Hard Crochet? Did it bear out the thinking of my textile-wise friend. What did stiffening and shrinking have to do, if anything, with felting? I flipped back to the Index and looked up "felt." The section of the book I was referred to described the scale structure of wool and something called unidirectional migration of filaments. Synthetic fibers, it was further explained, do not have scales and do not migrate unidirectionally, but "fortunately for the would-be felter some of the man-made fibres will shrink, and if a bundle of such fibres are caused to shrink the bundle shrinks too. . . . Any man-made fibre that shrinks appreciably, usually by treatment in hot water, can be made to felt."

End of story? Not quite. There was still an unresolved question: Was the modacrylic fiber that made up 30 percent of the yarn I used for Hard Crochet Dynel? Or was it one of the other three modacrylic fibers? A page or two later in the book I found the following passage: "Large quantities, running into hundreds of tons of Dynel, have been sold for carpets, where the Dynel is blended with an acrylic fibre to prevent the acrylic fibre flashing in the event of fire. As little as 30 percent Dynel in the blend will considerably reduce the fire risk."

It certainly seemed as if the book was talking about my yarn; Dynel must, I thought, be the answer. A little further on in the book, however, I read that Verel, one of the other modacrylics, is also used extensively in the manufacture of carpets and rugs. So, was I crocheting with Dynel or Verel or something else?

Dynel, Verel, whatever. I am convinced that no matter what the fiber is, the yarns that superblock so superstrong certainly do felt.

And what of Hard Crochet in the round? Why do these same yarns crochet so rigidly when worked in spiraling rounds? The book spoke of acrylics and acrylic/modacrylic blends in terms of their "tenacity," "elongation at break," "tensile strength," "extension," and "breaking length." Some of what was explained was fairly understandable; some of it was pretty deep. And I have to confess that after reading it all I really can't say for sure what it is that makes the yarns that crochet up so hard crochet up so hard; I only know that they do.

I also know that most people have a difficult time telling these yarns from natural wool. By no means an accident, this similarity is due to the fact that most acrylic yarns and blends, along with lots of other synthetic yarns, are *stapled*. The originally very long (sometimes miles long, according to Mr. Moncrieff) synthetic fiber strands are chopped into short filaments—like those occurring in natural yarns—which are then twisted together into yarns with the appearance and feel, or *handle*, of wool.

Are these acrylic/modacrylic blend carpet yarns the only synthetic yarns that crochet up hard? No indeed. The basket on page 89 is made with it, but the basket with the amazing weight-lifting ability on page 18 is worked in a synthetic yarn with a composition that to this day remains a mystery to me. In the back of *Man-Made Fibres*, there is a list of commercial synthetic fibers—*741 of them!* I'm sure quite a few of them would work up very well.

And what about natural yarns? Can any of them be crocheted rigidly enough to qualify as Hard Crochet yarns? So far, I haven't found any, but I haven't tried them all; so, who knows? There's still plenty of room for experimenting and lots of new discoveries just waiting to be made.

Gauge, Hook Size, and Stitch Size

After I had finished explaining to someone that gauge is simply a measure of the number of stitches per inch, the one I'd explained this to knowingly replied, "Oh, you mean how many stitches I can make out of an inch of yarn, right?" A most curious and interesting thought and one that deserved further investigating. But it had nothing at all to do with gauge.

Gauge, in crochet, is a measure of the number of finished stitches in a given distance, either horizontal or vertical. A seven-inch-wide piece of crochet with thirty-five stitches in each row has a horizontal gauge of five stitches to the inch. Vertical gauge is usually expressed in rows or rounds per inch.

Given the same weight of yarn, the higher the gauge (the more stitches to the inch), the tighter the crochet. Three-ply acrylic/modacrylic carpet yarn, for example, worked at a gauge of two stitches to the inch is very flimsy. At three stitches to the inch, the crochet is still fairly loose. When the gauge is increased to four stitches per inch, there is considerably more body; at six stitches per inch, the work starts to get truly rigid; a gauge of seven stitches to the inch (not always possible with every three-ply yarn) produces a material that's extremely hard and rigid. How do you get three-ply carpet yarn to crochet so tight that six or even seven stitches can fit into a space as small as an inch? You use a very small crochet hook, one normally used for crocheting much thinner yarn.

Crocheting three-ply yarn loosely with a small crochet hook is at best difficult; it takes a conscious effort to overcome the little hook's natural tendency to make little stitches. Working the same weight yarn tightly with a very large hook, with its own natural tendency to make large stitches, is next to impossible. Crochet hooks have a mind of their own: Give them a particular weight of yarn and, depending on the relative difference between hook size and yarn weight, they will crochet it either tightly or loosely.

Want to make very open and loose crochet out of very thin yarn? Use a large, fat crochet hook. Want to use fat, heavy yarn to make something tight? Use a small hook. It's as simple as that. And Hard Crochet is just that simple, too. Hard Crochet takes maximum advantage of a small yet strong crochet hook's natural tendency to make small, compact stitches. Crocheting hard and tight doesn't require all that much thinking—your hook does most of the thinking for you.

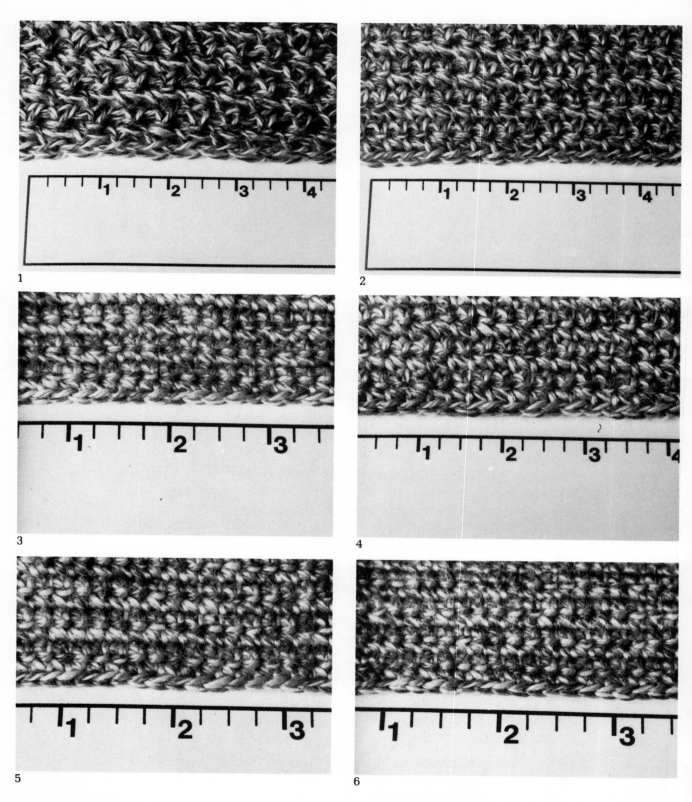

Three-ply carpet yarn crocheted at (1) 2 stitches to the inch, (2) 3 stitches to the inch, (3) 4 stitches to the inch, (4) 5 stitches to the inch, (5) 6 stitches to the inch, and (6) 7 stitches to the inch. PHOTOS BY THE AUTHOR.

Three-ply carpet yarn can also be used for crocheting loosely, as in this detail of a scarf by Diane Kender.

Making a Hook
with a Homemade Handle

Crochet hooks come in a wide range of sizes and are made from a number of different materials. The largest hooks are usually plastic or aluminum; the smallest hooks, because their size demands greater strength, are most often made of steel. Aluminum hooks and plastic hooks have no place in Hard Crochet. They are both too large and too weak.

Steel crochet hooks, the only kind suitable for Hard Crochet, range in size from the almost microscopic #14 (make sure if you buy a #14 that it really has a hook on the end) to the more substantial #00. Most Hard Crochet is done with a #1 steel hook (two sizes smaller than a #00)

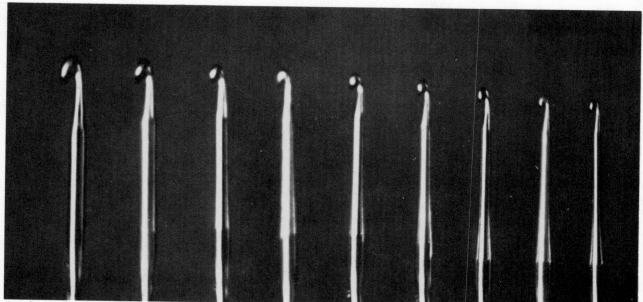

Steel crochet hooks. From left to right: Size 00, Size 0, Size 1, Size 2, Size 3, Size 4, Size 5, Size 6, Size 7. Sizes 8 through 14 are not shown.

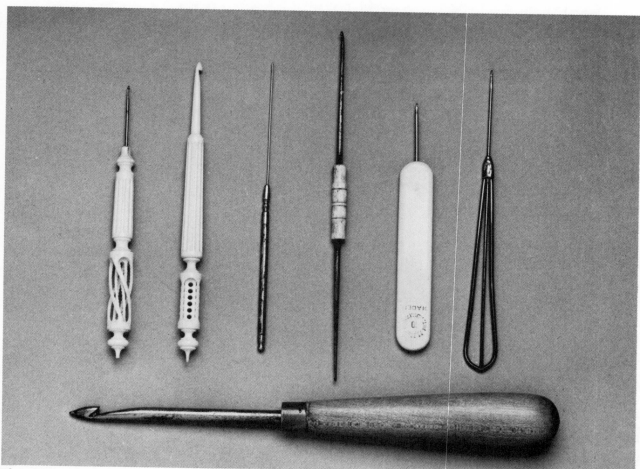

There was a time when almost all crochet hooks had nice, gripable handles. The large hook on the bottom is a rug hook. The second hook from the right is from the collection of Barbara Muccio; the rest belong to the author.

and occasionally with a #0. There's just one thing wrong with these otherwise perfect hooks: Their handles are much too narrow.

How well you are able to grip or hold a tool has a lot to do with how well you are able to control it, and the same holds true for a crochet hook, especially for a hook that's being used to crochet hard. Hard Crochet requires a high degree of hook control, and a sure, firm grip on the hook is absolutely essential.

In my search for a way to improve my grip on the crochet hook, I experimented with dozens of different homemade handles and finally settled on the design shown here. It's easy to make, takes only a short time, and uses materials commonly found around the house: masking tape (½, ¾, or 1 inch), a single-edge razor blade or Xacto-type knife, scrap fabric (cotton, lightweight denim, or any other material of similar weight that does not fray easily), a sewing needle, and heavy-duty thread. From these humble ingredients alone you can fashion a most impressive-looking homemade handle that should last as long as the hook.

To provide any hook with a homemade handle, first, holding a strip of masking tape perpendicular to the hook, fasten the end of the tape to the flattened finger-hold part of the hook (Fig. 1). Keeping tension on the tape, slowly rotate the hook so that the tape begins to wrap around it. Neatness counts here—the neater you wrap, the better the finished handle will be. Wrap until the taped area is as wide as a standard pencil (Fig. 2). Cut the tape and secure the short end.

Masking tape, cloth, and a needle and thread are all it takes to turn an ordinary steel crochet hook into an impressively powerful tool.

FIGURE 1

FIGURE 2

Attach the next tape strip end right next to the first wrap (Fig. 3), and wrap it around the hook until the second taped area is exactly as wide as the first. Continue making wraps until the entire hook handle is covered (Fig. 4). Don't worry if the last wrap goes beyond the end of the hook (Fig. 5), because the next step in the handle-making process will eliminate any such excess.

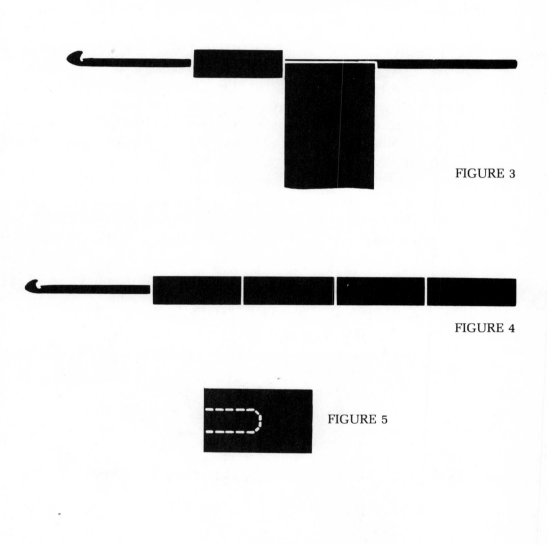

FIGURE 3

FIGURE 4

FIGURE 5

FIGURE 6

The next step is to take the single-edge razor blade or the Xacto knife and *very carefully* trim each wrap all around so they look like those in Figure 6. Trim the last wrap just enough to expose the very tip of the hook handle (Fig. 7).

FIGURE 7

Lay the hook on a strip of fabric that has been cut just wide enough to wrap around the hook with about a quarter-inch overlap, no more, and long enough to extend about a half inch beyond the first wrap and about an inch beyond the last wrap (Fig. 8).

Thread a needle with a doubled and knotted strand of heavy-duty thread. Wrap the fabric around the handle (Fig. 9), and insert the needle through the overlapping fabric sides at the point of the notch between the first and second tape wraps (Fig. 10). Pull the thread tight, and

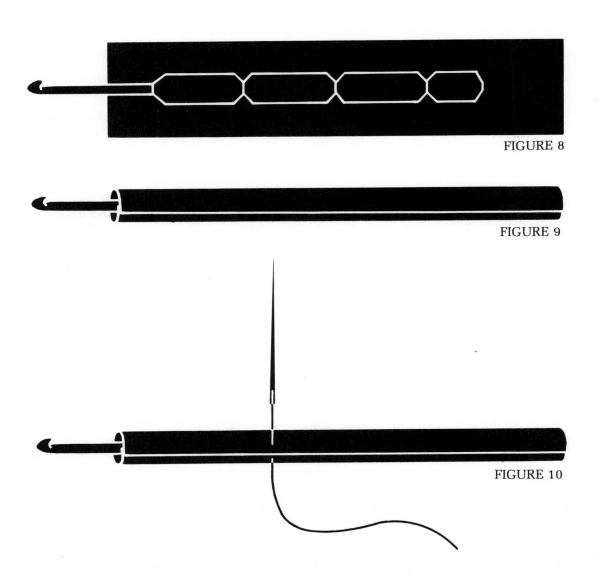

FIGURE 8

FIGURE 9

FIGURE 10

then wind it twice around the hook so the fabric conforms to the shape of the notch (Fig. 11). Secure the thread with a stitch in the notch, and then stitch the fabric around the hook in the following manner: Stitch up to the front of the hook and then once around the shank (Fig. 12); stitch back in the direction of the end of the hook, wrapping the thread around each notch as you go; neatly stitch the fabric at the end of the hook closed; stitch back to the point on the handle where the sewing began, fasten off the thread, and trim excess fabric from both ends of the hook (Fig. 13).

Use wrapped hooks for all practice work and while learning techniques, even when working loosely. This will help you to get accustomed to working with a hook with a homemade handle.

One final note on crochet hooks: If you look closely at different brands of crochet hooks, you will notice that the hook heads on some of them have sharp edges (Fig. 14). Never buy this kind of hook for Hard Crochet; buy only hooks with smooth, contoured hook heads (Fig. 15).

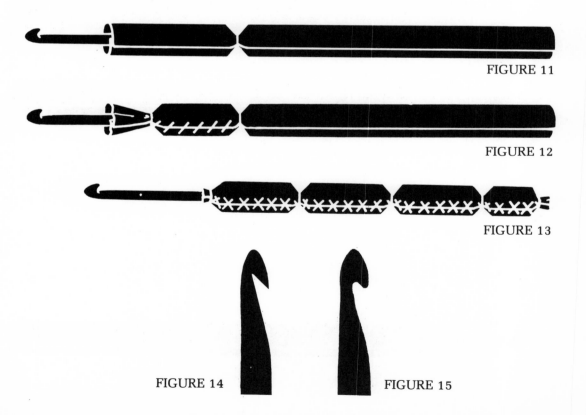

FIGURE 11

FIGURE 12

FIGURE 13

FIGURE 14   FIGURE 15

How Difficult Is Hard Crochet?

Hard Crochet isn't just for Mr. Universe types with large, hairy forearms extending up to great, big, bulging, body-beautiful biceps. And you don't have to go around crushing beer cans to get your hands in shape. The average person's hands already possess more than enough strength to crochet hard.

Have you ever tied your shoelaces and, daydreaming, broken a brand-new lace? That's hand strength, hand strength without the help of a tool like a crochet hook and the leverage it uses. Using that leverage to the maximum benefit is really what makes Hard Crochet possible.

Hard Crochet isn't all that difficult; just knowing that it is possible is perhaps half the battle.

CROCHET: THE BASICS AND BEYOND

How to Hold the Crochet Hook

A very old and popular way to hold a crochet hook is to hold it the way one normally grips a pencil. While this method is used by a large number, perhaps even a majority, of crocheters, holding the hook in this manner for Hard Crochet is completely out of the question. If you already hold your hook this way, you will have to give it up and learn the *palm grip* (Fig. 16), the only proper grip for Hard Crochet.

FIGURE 16

Basic Stitches and Techniques

There are dozens of different crochet stitches, ranging from very simple ones to the very complex and ornate. Hard Crochet employs only a handful of the most basic stitches: the *Chain Stitch*—the stitch used to create the starting foundation for all crochet, for reversing directions, for making "holes" in crochet work, and for other important functions; the *Single Crochet Stitch*—the simplest of the crochet pattern stitches and the basic working

33

FIGURE 17

stitch in Hard Crochet; the *Double Crochet Stitch*—a stitch that's twice as high as Single Crochet and used only occasionally in Hard Crochet; the *Half Double Crochet Stitch*—shorter than Double Crochet and taller than Single Crochet, a stitch used to make transitions between the two; the *Slip Stitch*—a very handy little stitch most often used for joining other stitches and similar "mechanical" chores. Because they are the only ones used in Hard Crochet, how to make only these five stitches will be covered in the pages that follow.

Before going on, take a #00 steel crochet hook and provide it with a homemade handle. Then select some three-ply carpet yarn, preferably the acrylic carpet yarn mentioned earlier.

FIGURE 18

MAKING A SLIP KNOT

Making a *Slip Knot* is the first step in beginning any piece of crochet work—from it emerges the *foundation chain*.

To make a Slip Knot, follow the steps shown in Figures 17 through 21. Once the Slip Knot is made, insert the hook end of the crochet hook into and through the open loop. Pull the short yarn end so that the loop closes around the hook (Fig. 22), but not too tightly; the hook should be able to slide easily.

FIGURE 19

FIGURE 20

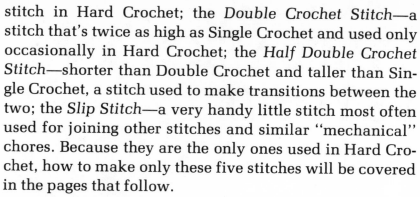

FIGURE 21

34

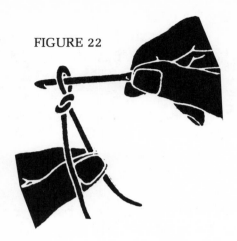

FIGURE 22

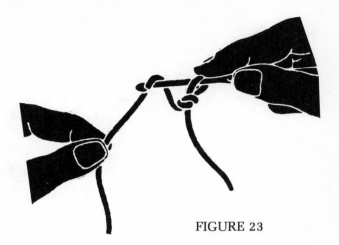

FIGURE 23

Holding the hook with the grip described earlier, slide the Slip Knot loop a short way up the hook and hold it there with your index finger. Then take the long end of the yarn and bring it up and over the hook (Fig. 23). This maneuver is appropriately called *yarning over.*

You must yarn over *from the back of the hook to the front* (Fig. 24), never from the front to the back (Fig. 25).

Take the long yarn end and hold it between the fingers of your left hand (Fig. 26). Then take hold of the Slip Knot just below the loop with the thumb and index finger of your left hand (Fig. 27). Keep the long yarn end yarned over the hook. You are ready to make Chain Stitches.

FIGURE 24

FIGURE 25

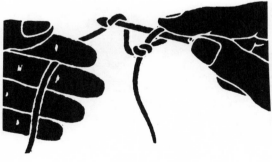

FIGURE 26

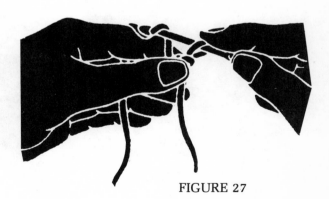

FIGURE 27

MAKING A CHAIN

Pull the long yarn end through the loop on the hook (Fig. 28). You have just *yarned through*. And you made a Chain Stitch. Yarn over and yarn through again. There's another Chain Stitch.

Keep some tension on the long yarn end as you allow it to slide through your fingers as each new Chain Stitch is made. And keep some downward tension on the chain as it develops and gets longer (Fig. 29).

With practice, your Chain Stitches will soon become very even and regular. Make a few practice chains, some with fairly loose stitches, some with fairly tight stitches. Try to develop some control over the tightness of the stitches as you crochet them.

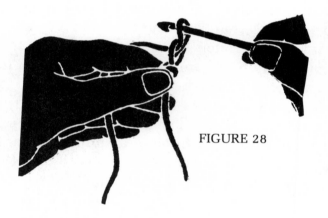

FIGURE 28

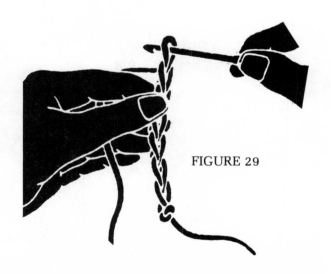

FIGURE 29

RIPPING OUT

Crochet has one big advantage over most other fiber crafts: Mistakes, when spotted early enough, can be very easily undone and corrected.

Make a short, not-too-tight chain. Remove the hook from the last chain loop and pull the long yarn end. The stitches in the chain should pull right out. This is called *ripping out*, and it's a bona fide technique used over and over again by crocheters for undoing crochet errors. All crochet stitches, no matter how complex, can be ripped out.

Working into the Chain: Two Different Ways

Once the *foundation chain* has reached the desired length (number of stitches), it can be crocheted into. Working back over the chain, new stitches are worked into each of the stitches along its length. This can be done in one of two ways.

Figure 30 shows how a hook is inserted into the "front" of a foundation chain. Inserting the hook into the "back" of the chain is shown in Figure 31.

Working into the back of a chain makes for a more finished, neater edge, called a *finished chain edge*, but it's a bit more difficult than working into the front of a chain. Practice working into a foundation chain both ways; while learning new stitches and techniques, though, use the first and easier method.

FIGURE 30

FIGURE 31

FIGURE 32

SINGLE CROCHET

Chain 15. This means make a chain fifteen Chain Stitches long, *not* including the Slip Knot loop. Hold the chain as shown in Figure 32. The arrow is indicating the second chain from the hook, the place in a foundation chain where the first Single Crochet is always made.

Working into the front of the chain, insert the hook into and through the second chain from the hook (Fig. 33). Then yarn over (Fig. 34). And yarn through (Fig. 35). There are now two loops on the hook. Yarn over once more (Fig. 36), and yarn through both loops (Fig. 37) to complete the first Single Crochet. Notice that there is now only one loop left on the hook. You are ready to make the next Single Crochet in the next stitch in the chain (indicated by the arrow in Fig. 37). Insert the hook into and

FIGURE 33

FIGURE 34

FIGURE 36

FIGURE 35

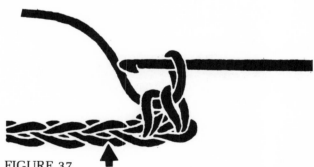

FIGURE 37

through the chain; yarn over; yarn through (there should again be two loops on the hook); yarn over once more; and yarn through both loops to finish the second Single Crochet. Continue making Single Crochets to the end of the foundation chain (Fig. 38).

After the last stitch has been made in the last stitch of the foundation chain (the original Slip Knot loop), chain 1. That means make a Chain Stitch by yarning over and yarning through the loop on the hook (Fig. 39). This is called the *turning chain.*

You are now ready to turn the piece of work around and work a new row of Singles back over the row just completed. Turn the work so that the back of the first row of Single Crochet is facing you (Fig. 40). (The "back" of a stitch is the side facing *away from you as you make it.*)

(Regardless of what some crocheters and crochet books tell you, the direction in which you turn the work—clockwise or counterclockwise—is unimportant. But you should be consistent about the direction you turn it.)

The arrow in Figure 40 points to the *first stitch in the previous row,* the stitch into which the first Single Crochet of a new row is made.

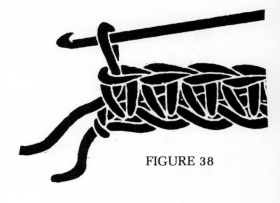

FIGURE 38

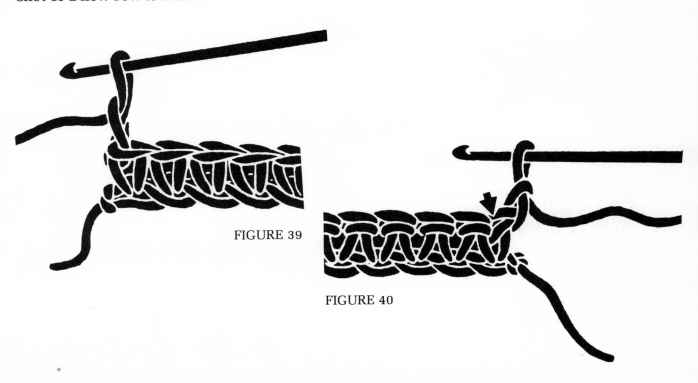

FIGURE 39

FIGURE 40

FIGURE 41

FIGURE 42

FIGURE 43

FIGURE 44

FIGURE 45

HOW TO INSERT A HOOK INTO STITCHES

Knowing the different ways and places to insert the crochet hook when making stitches is important, and this is as good a place as any to stop and consider them.

When working rows of stitches back and forth, new stitches are always worked into the stitches in the previous row *from the back* (Fig. 41). The hook is inserted into and through the spaces indicated by the dots in Figure 42 and, unless otherwise indicated, under the full loop at the top of the stitch (Fig. 43).

When working rows of stitches in the round (see "Crocheting in the Round," pages 49–51), new stitches are worked into the previous row's stitches *from the front* (Fig. 44). The hook is inserted into and through the spaces indicated by the dots in Figure 45, and unless directed to do otherwise, under the full loop at the top of the stitch (Fig. 46).

Instructions will sometimes tell you to work into the "back loop," or simply "the back," of each stitch in a previous row (Fig. 47), or into the "front loop," or "the front," of each stitch in the previous row (Fig. 48).

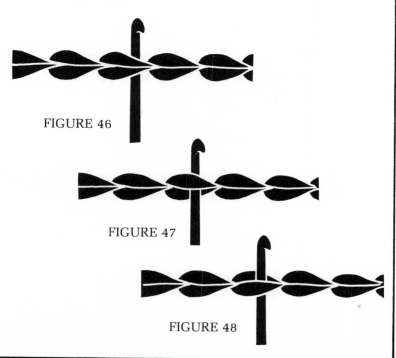

FIGURE 46

FIGURE 47

FIGURE 48

Insert the hook into and through the first stitch in the previous row (Fig. 49); yarn over; yarn through; yarn over again; and yarn through to complete the first stitch in the new row. Continue making Singles until you come to the end of the row. Once there, chain 1, turn the work around, and work another row of Single Crochet back over the previous one. Make another row, and then another; continue making back-and-forth rows of Single Crochet until what you have is a piece of material measuring about twice as long as it is wide. When the work is long enough, *fasten off* (see following instructions).

Examine what you have crocheted. The last row probably looks a lot better, more uniform and regular, than the first few rows. For practice and review, make another chain and then more rows of Single Crochet, working them until you have another piece of crochet like the first one you made. Compare the two; you should notice a good deal of improvement. Keep practicing until making even, regular stitches becomes an automatic and effortless operation.

FIGURE 49

FASTENING OFF

When you decide to end a piece of crochet after working the desired number of rows, you will need to fasten off the last stitch in the last row so that it, and all the stitches before it, can't and won't rip out.

To fasten off, cut the yarn, leaving an end three or four inches long (Fig. 50). Then yarn over and yarn through, pulling the yarn end all the way through the loop on the hook (Fig. 51). Pull the yarn end to make it fast (Fig. 52).

FIGURE 50

FIGURE 51

FIGURE 52

DOUBLE CROCHET

Make another chain a dozen or more stitches long. Work a row of Single Crochet back over the chain and stop at the end of the row. Instead of chaining 1 before turning the work, chain 3 (Fig. 53), and then turn the piece around and yarn over (Fig. 54).

Since the turning chain in Double Crochet counts as a stitch, the first Double Crochet is made in the *second stitch in the previous row* (indicated by the arrow in Fig. 54).

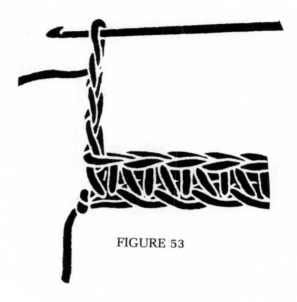

FIGURE 53

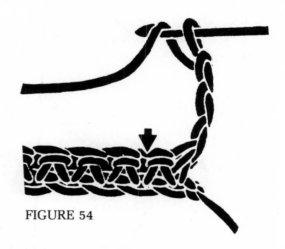

FIGURE 54

With the yarn yarned securely over it, insert the hook into and through the second stitch in the previous row (Fig. 55). Then yarn over (Fig. 56) and yarn through (Fig. 57). After yarning through, there will be three loops on the hook. Yarn over and yarn through only *two* of the

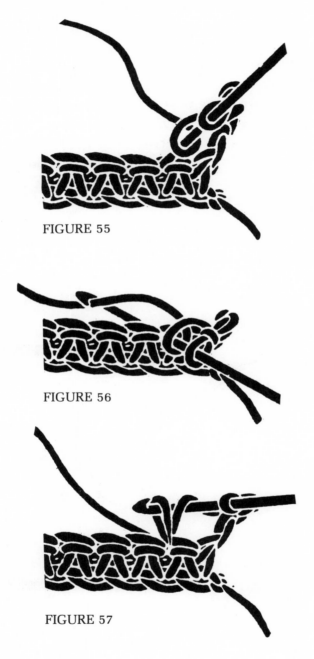

FIGURE 55

FIGURE 56

FIGURE 57

loops on the hook—two loops will remain (Fig. 58). Yarn over and yarn through the two remaining loops (Fig. 59). That completes the first Double Crochet.

Make another Double Crochet in the next stitch: Yarn over; insert the hook into and through the stitch in the previous row; yarn over; yarn through; yarn over; yarn through only the first two loops on the hook; yarn over again; and yarn through the last two loops. Continue making Doubles to the end of the row. When the last stitch is finished, chain 3, turn, and work another row of Doubles back over the first. (Remember to make the first Double in the second stitch in the previous row.) When you reach the end of this row—the first row of Double Crochet worked into another row of Double Crochet— make the last stitch in the row into the top of the turning chain that started the previous row (Fig. 60).

To start a row of Double Crochet into a foundation chain, yarn over and make the first stitch in the *fourth* chain from the hook (Fig. 61).

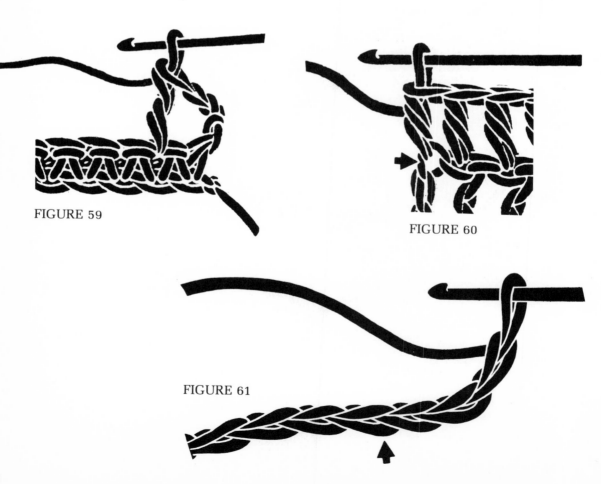

FIGURE 58

FIGURE 59

FIGURE 60

FIGURE 61

HALF DOUBLE CROCHET

Make another 12-stitch-long chain and work a row of Single Crochet back over it. After completing the last Single Crochet in the row, chain 2, and turn. Just as it does for Double Crochet, the turning chain in Half Double Crochet counts as the first stitch in the row; therefore, the first Half Double Crochet will be made in the *second stitch in the previous row.*

The first steps in making a Half Double Crochet are exactly the same as for Double Crochet: Yarn over; insert the hook into and through the stitch in the previous row; yarn over; and yarn through. At this point, there should be three loops on the hook (Fig. 62). Now, instead of yarning through only the first two loops, yarn through *all the loops on the hook,* all three of them (Fig. 63).

That's how the shorter Half Double Crochet is made. Work Half Doubles to the end of the row, chain 2 (it's 1 for Single and 2 for Double), turn, make another row of Half Doubles and then a few more.

At the end of one of the rows, chain only 1 before turning and begin the next row with a Single Crochet. Finish the row with the following sequence of stitches: a Half Double; a Double; a Half Double; a Single; a Half Double; a Double; a Half Double; a Single, and so on to the end of the row. The Half Double Crochets in this row are used as transition stitches between the shorter Singles and taller Doubles in the row.

FIGURE 62

FIGURE 63

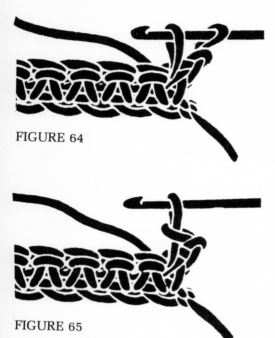

FIGURE 64

FIGURE 65

THE SLIP STITCH

Make another chain and then work three or four rows of Single Crochet. At the end of the last row of Singles, chain 1 and turn. As if you were starting another row of Single Crochet, insert your hook into and through the first stitch in the previous row. Yarn over and yarn through the stitch (Fig. 64) *and* through the loop on the hook (Fig. 65). Do it again: Insert the hook into and through the next stitch; yarn over; then yarn through both the stitch and the loop on the hook. That's the Slip Stitch.

Slip Stitches are kind of like *Half* Singles (the French call a Slip Stitch a Single Crochet and a Single Crochet a Double Crochet). They can also be thought of as Chain Stitches made "around" or into another stitch.

Slip Stitches are rarely used for straight, row-upon-row crocheting. They are used instead for joining rounds of crochet worked in other stitches, for fastening off stitches, and as a step in making other stitches.

INCREASING AND DECREASING

Crochet work may be widened by *increasing* the number of stitches in a row or round. To make an increase, simply work two stitches into any stitch in the previous row (Fig. 66).

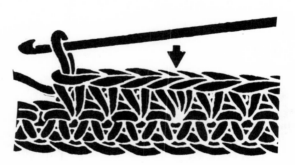

FIGURE 66

If you increase at a gradual and regular rate—one increase every other row, for instance—and stagger the increases, the resulting shape will look something like the one represented in Figure 67 (the little dots represent staggered increases).

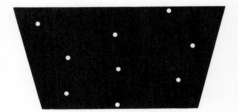

FIGURE 67

Increases can also be made at either the beginning of a row or at the end of a row. If regular increases are made at the end or beginning of rows and on only one side of the piece of crochet, the shape will end up looking something like the one in Figure 68 (again, the dots are the increases). The side with no increases remains unaffected.

FIGURE 68

Make a few practice swatches, increasing both at the sides and within rows. And alter the rate of increase—an increase every row will cause the crochet to widen twice as rapidly as increasing only every other row.

While increasing widens and expands the dimensions of crochet, *decreasing* does just the opposite. You decrease by eliminating stitches from the work.

Make a chain about a dozen stitches long and then work a row of Single Crochet back over it. Turn; make 5 more Singles; insert the hook into and through the next stitch; yarn over and yarn through the stitch; and *stop* (Fig. 69). Now, insert the hook into and through the next stitch in the row; yarn over and yarn back through the stitch. You should have three loops on the hook (Fig. 70). Yarn over and yarn through all three loops (Fig. 71).

FIGURE 70

FIGURE 71

Where there had been two stitches in the previous row there is now only one stitch. Continue on by making Singles in the remaining stitches in the row.

Like increasing, decreasing can be done anywhere in a row—at the beginning, at the end, or in the middle. Regular decreases scattered throughout a piece of crochet will cause it to narrow at a regular, even rate, as in the shape represented in Figure 72. Regular decreases made on only one side of the work will cause the shape to narrow as in Figure 73.

You can increase forever and the crochet will just get wider and wider, but you can decrease down to the point where there are no stitches left to decrease. This is the common way to make triangle shapes in crochet (Fig. 74). When the last stitch in such a triangle has been made, fasten off.

Practice decreasing at the end of rows, at the beginning of rows, and in the middle of rows.

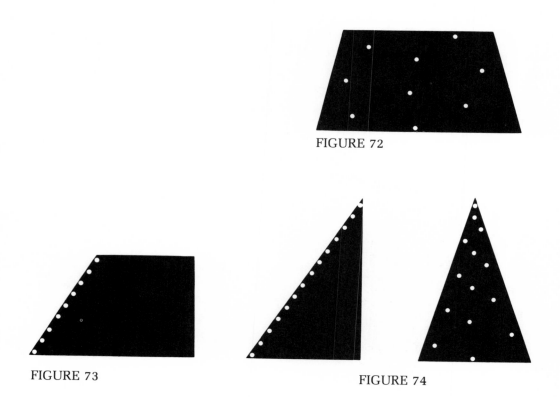

FIGURE 72

FIGURE 73

FIGURE 74

CROCHETING IN THE ROUND

If instead of crocheting in back-and-forth rows, you connect the ends of a foundation chain so it has no beginning and no end, you will find that you're able to crochet in spiraling rows called *rounds*. Work a few rounds and they turn into a tube.

To learn to make such a tube, chain about 20. Insert the hook into and through the first stitch (the Slip Knot loop) in the chain (Fig. 75), yarn over and then through both the chain and the loop on the hook (Fig. 76). You have just connected the ends of the chain with a Slip Stitch.

Insert the hook into and through the next stitch in the chain; yarn over; yarn through the chain; yarn over again; and yarn through the loops on the hook. That makes the first Single worked in the chain (Fig. 77). Work a Single in each chain loop. When you arrive back at the point where the first Single was made in the chain, make a Single into it and continue crocheting around, working into each stitch in the previous round. Continue working in this fashion until you have a tube about four inches tall (Fig. 78), and then fasten off.

There's another way to crochet in the round. If you make a very short chain, connect its ends, and then crochet around with frequent increases, a flat, disclike shape called a *flat round* will result.

FIGURE 75

FIGURE 76

FIGURE 78

FIGURE 77

To start a flat round, chain only 4, join the ends of the chain with a Slip Stitch, and then increase (make 2 Singles) into each chain. Continuing around, increase into each stitch in the round below until the outside rim of the flat round contains 24 stitches (Fig. 79). Work the next round even (no increases). When you have completed the even round, make another increase round, increasing in every *other* stitch: increase; no increase; increase, no increase; increase; and so on. Follow this round with another even round. Follow the even round with another increase round, increasing this time in every *third* stitch: increase; no increase; no increase; increase; no increase; no increase; increase; and so on. Keep working rounds in the following fashion; an even round; an increase round (every *fifth* stitch); an even round; an increase round (every *sixth* stitch); an even round; an increase round (every *seventh* stitch); and so on. Work a few more rounds this way and then fasten off.

Count the increases in each increase round. There should be 12 increases in each. Twelve increases in every

FIGURE 79

Each of these little flat rounds was worked with 12 increases in each increase round. The middle disc is a little tighter than the disc on the left, and not quite as tight as the disc on the right. Thirteen increases per increase round might have kept the middle disc flat; 14 increases in each of its increase rounds would have done the same for the disc on the right.

increase round (when every other round is an increase round) will keep most flat rounds nice and flat. Very tightly worked crochet, however, sometimes requires 13 or even 14 increases per increase round to keep a flat round flat. (If you're making a flat round that requires 13 increases in each increase round, keep increasing in every stitch at the beginning of the work until you have 26 stitches around the edge. An increase in every other stitch in the next increase round will give you the desired 13 increases. To start a flat round that will need 14 increases per round, work increases in every stitch until there are 28 stitches all around.)

What happens if you increase too frequently, making too many increases in each increase round? Instead of staying flat, the crochet will become wavy; its edges will ruffle. Too few increases? Instead of staying flat, the edges of the disc will begin to turn up all around.

Practice making flat rounds. Working into the chain and making the first few rounds is both the most difficult and the most important part of making a flat round. Practice these beginning steps until the working becomes easy and the work even and neat.

JOINING ROUNDS

You may have noticed how fastening off at the end of tubes and flat rounds left the last round of stitches standing conspicuously above the round below it. A technique called *joining rounds* eliminates this effect.

When rounds are joined, the beginning of each new round is "stepped up" (Fig. 80), so the last stitches in the round run into and join up with the front of the round (Fig. 81). When the join is made, the next stepped-up round is begun.

FIGURE 80

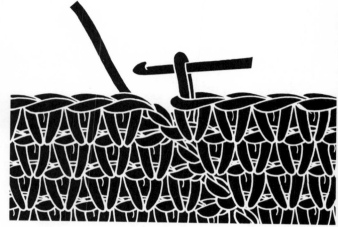

FIGURE 81

To learn how to join rounds, make a chain about 25 stitches long and join the ends. Work Singles around and stop when the last Single in the chain is done (Fig. 82). Slip stitch into the next stitch (the first Single in the chain) and chain 1 (Fig. 83). Make a Single in the next and all stitches around. When you reach the point where you made the Slip Stitch, *skip it* (don't work into the Slip Stitch loop) and slip stitch into the next stitch, the first stitch in the previous round. Then chain 1 (Fig. 84). Each time around skip the Slip Stitch loop, slip stitch into the first Single in the previous round, and chain 1 (the chain loop becomes the top of the first Single).

You don't necessarily have to begin joining rounds with the first round out of the starting chain; you can be-

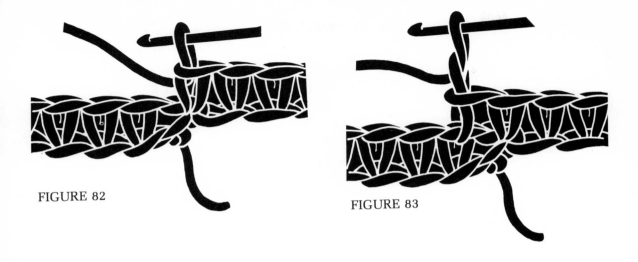

FIGURE 82

FIGURE 83

FIGURE 84

gin joining at any time. At the point where you would like
to begin joining rounds—like six or so rounds before you
fasten off the last round in a tube so the rounds join up to
make a nice, even rim—simply slip stitch into the next
stitch in the previous round, chain 1, and make a Single
in the next and all stitches around. When you arrive back
at the Slip Stitch loop, skip it, slip stitch into the next
stitch, chain 1, and then work Singles into the next and
the rest of the stitches in the round. After two or three
rounds have been joined in this manner, both ends of the
rounds should be on about the same level.

When the time comes to fasten off, just join the ends of
the round with a Slip Stitch, clip the yarn, yarn the end
over and all the way through the loop on the hook. The

FIGURE 85

result (Fig. 85) will look nothing like the conspicuous fastening-off points on the tubes with unjoined rounds made earlier.

You can also join a flat round's rounds. Don't begin joining rounds until the beginning of the first even round. After the last increase in the round preceding the first even round has been made, slip stitch into the next stitch, chain 1, make a Single (the first Single of the even round) in the next stitch, and then continue around. Join each of the flat round's rounds the same way you joined the tube's rounds.

SHAPING FLAT ROUNDS
(SO THEY DON'T STAY SO FLAT)

Remember what happens when you make a flat round with too few increases per increase round? If you recall, the edges of the disc begin to turn up all around. If you stop increasing altogether, the edges turn up very quickly; you soon find yourself crocheting a tube—a tube connected to a flat, closed-off bottom. How would you describe a basket to someone who has never seen one? How about a tube with a flat, closed-off bottom? And what's the simplest way to explain what a hat crown is? All the baskets and worked-in-the-round hats in this book started out as simple flat rounds.

To make a simple basket shape, first make a flat round that measures around three inches across. Stop increasing but continue working rounds. After about three rounds, the edges of the flat round should begin to turn up noticeably (Fig. 86). Work a dozen more rounds. The end product should be a little basket shape like the one in Figure 87.

When you simply stop increasing, the flat round turns up abruptly. But a gradual reduction in the rate of increase, spread over a number of rounds, will result in a more gently curved turnup, as in Figure 88. Practice making flat rounds and turning them up.

FIGURE 86

FIGURE 87

FIGURE 88

Basket shapes can be manipulated still further. If you want the top of a basket to flare out (see Fig. 89), for example, start increasing again at the point where you would like the flaring out to begin. The greater the increase rate, of course, the more rapidly the rim will turn out. To make a basket's rim turn in (see Fig. 90), work a few decrease rounds. The number and frequency of decreases will determine how sharply the rim turns in.

Combining increase rounds with decrease rounds can result in some fairly complicated basket shapes; the shape outlined in Figure 91 is an example. This shape would result from a slightly gradual reduction of a flat round's increase rate, two or three no-increase rounds, a number of rounds with a few increases in each round, two or three more even rounds, quite a few decrease rounds, many even rounds (the long neck), and a few final increase rounds. Notice the resemblance between this shape and the basket on page 105.

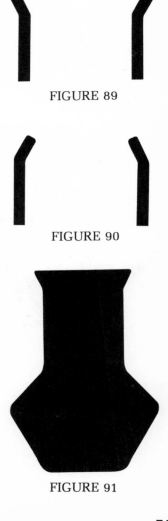

FIGURE 89

FIGURE 90

FIGURE 91

As you make more and more basket shapes, you will gain greater control over the way they develop. These practice basket shapes don't have to be crocheted very tightly; however, the tighter you make them, the more they will become truly basketlike.

TYING ON NEW YARN

When a change of yarn is needed—to switch to a different color or to add a new length of yarn to a yarn that's about to run out—there are a number of ways you can make the change.

When working in back-and-forth rows, new yarn is usually added at the end of a row. Take two colors of the same weight yarn and begin working with one of them. Chain 15, work a row of Single Crochet back over the chain, and then crochet five or six more rows. At the end of the last row, stop just short of yarning through to complete the last stitch in the row; there should be two loops on the hook (Fig. 92). Without removing the hook, clip the yarn a few inches from the work. Take a new yarn and tie it to the old yarn, as in Figure 93, using a square knot and making the knot as close to the stitch as possible. Yarn the new color over the hook and yarn it through both loops on the hook (Fig. 94). Chain 1, turn, and work the new row with the new color.

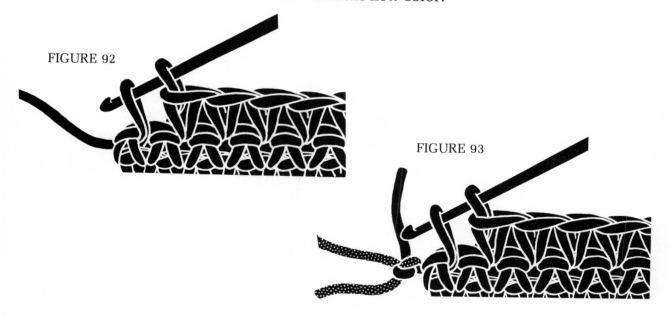

FIGURE 92

FIGURE 93

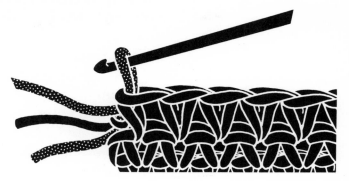

FIGURE 94

Sometimes you have to tie on a new length of yarn (usually the same yarn) in the middle of a row or round. To do so, simply stop working at a point where there are two loops on the hook (Fig. 95). Without removing the hook, clip the old length of yarn two or three inches from the stitch, tie on the new length of yarn (Fig. 96), yarn over with the new yarn, yarn it through the two loops on the hook, and then continue crocheting with the new length of yarn. Knots, by the way, should always be made on the side of the work that isn't going to be seen, on the so-called wrong side of the crochet.

FIGURE 95

FIGURE 96

Tying on a new color in the round is done in a very different way. Make a tube about two inches high, joining rounds as you crochet. (You should always be joining your rounds when color changes are anticipated.) Finish the last round, join the ends of the round with a Slip Stitch, clip the yarn two or three inches from the stitch, and fasten off the end (Fig. 97). An inch or two behind the fastened-off end, tie on the new color (Fig. 98). Insert the hook into and through the stitch the new yarn is tied to, yarn over and yarn the new yarn through the stitch, and chain 1. Insert the hook back into and through the *same* stitch, yarn over again, yarn back through the stitch (you should have two loops on the hook), and yarn through both loops. You are now ready to continue. Crochet along and then, as neatly as possible, right over the old join and fasten-off point. Continue joining rounds with the new yarn in this manner: Complete the last stitch in the round; slip stitch into the top of the stitch at the tie-on point; chain 1, and continue around.

FIGURE 97

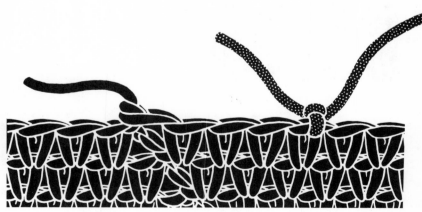

FIGURE 98

58

HIDING YARN ENDS

Tying on new yarn at the end of a row left loose yarn ends, as did tying on new yarn in the middle of a row and a new color in the round. And every time you fasten off, you're left with a loose end that has to be secured and hidden from view.

There are two basic ways to deal with loose yarn ends: (1) using a needle or a crochet hook, you can either sew or hook them into the work when the piece of crochet is finished, or (2) you can crochet right over loose ends, securing and concealing them as they occur.

The first method calls for threading a blunt-nosed needle with the loose yarn end and then sewing it into the work. Or, if you prefer, you can work the loose end into the crochet with a small crochet hook, pulling the end through five or six stitches to secure it (Fig. 99). Whatever you choose to do, all yarn-end hiding should be done in the back of the work.

FIGURE 99

Crocheting right over yarn ends as they occur can save you from the tedium of having to secure lots of loose ends later. When a new yarn is tied on at the end of a row, instead of leaving the two ends hanging loose, hold them flat against the back of the work and crochet right over them, making them secure. Secure loose ends that occur in the middle of a row and in the round the same way.

BORDERING CROCHET

Examine the sides of a sample of back-and-forth crochet, the sides where all the chaining and turning took place. No matter how neat you work, these sides will always have a somewhat rough look to them. Raw edges like these can be given a more finished appearance by bordering them with a row of crochet.

Make a sample swatch of Single Crochet; make it about thirty stitches wide and around thirty rows high. Fasten off at the end of the last row. Take a new length of yarn—a contrasting color will make it easier for you to see what's happening—and tie it to the top of a stitch somewhere in the middle of the last row. With the side of the work facing you that allows you to crochet in the direction of the fastened-off yarn end, insert the hook into and through the stitch you tied to, yarn over and yarn back through, chain 1, insert the hook back into and through the *same* stitch, yarn over and yarn through, and then yarn through the two loops on the hook. Crochet over the loose yarn end for four or five stitches to secure it behind the work; work Singles in the direction of the fastened-off end of the row. When you are five stitches from the loose end, take it and crochet it in behind the work. In the last stitch in the row, make a *double increase*—work three stitches into the one (Fig. 100). (A double increase is always necessary when a 90-degree corner has to be turned, a frequent occurrence when bordering crochet.) You are now ready to crochet into the raw side of the swatch.

There are natural spaces in the side into which stitches can be made. These *natural stitch spaces* are "between" the rows of stitches and in the "ends" of rows; they are indicated by the little white dots in Figure 101.

Before you begin to work into the side, consider the following: At what gauge are you going to crochet into the side? Is the row gauge (the number of rows to the inch measuring vertically) exactly the same as the stitch gauge (the number of stitches to the inch measuring horizontally)? If it were, you could crochet into each natural stitch space without having to worry about maintaining the proper gauge. Any difference between the two gauges should be compensated for, equalized by either increasing or decreasing as you work into the side. When all the work is being done in Single Crochet, it is safe to assume that the row gauge will be a little lower than the horizontal stitch gauge (fewer rows per inch than stitches per

FIGURE 100

FIGURE 101

inch), and this difference in gauge is usually the same for both tight and loose Single Crochet. The ratio is roughly six (stitches to the inch) to five (rows to the inch). To compensate, therefore, increase in every *sixth* natural stitch space.

Now, begin crocheting into the side, in the spaces between rows and in the ends of rows. Increase in every sixth space. When you reach the last stitch space, make a double increase into it and turn the corner.

You will now be crocheting into the foundation chain. Crochet along the bottom of the chain, make a double increase in the first stitch in the chain, turn the corner, and crochet into the remaining side. Turn the final corner, and crochet up to and join into the first stitch in the border. Can you count the number of new techniques used in that one little border?

Practice by crocheting borders around some of your early sample work. Make a double border around one of them: Just go around twice. Remember to double increase at each corner; but you can forget about increasing in every sixth stitch along the sides—you already adjusted the gauge the first time around.

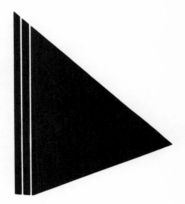

FIGURE 102

JOINING SEPARATE SECTIONS OF CROCHET

Separate sections of crochet are often joined together to create more complex shapes and objects. The body of the attaché case on page 141, for example, was made by attaching two crocheted rectangles (the sides of the case) to a long narrow piece of crochet (the gusset). Crochet sections can be joined by either stitching or crocheting their edges together. Separate pieces of Hard Crochet, because of their extremely tight stitches, are usually sewn or stitched together. To stitch crocheted pieces, use a blunt-nosed needle and the same yarn used in the crochet.

If you want two sections to be back-to-back after they are joined (Fig. 102), place them *back-to-back,* line up the stitches to be joined (Fig. 103), and stitch through both loops in each row (Fig. 104).

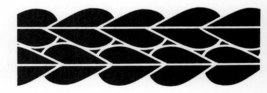

FIGURE 103

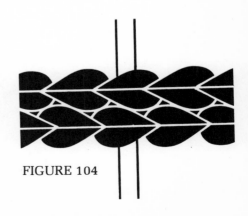

FIGURE 104

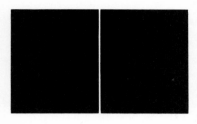

FIGURE 105

If you want the pieces to line up next to each other edge-to-edge after they are joined (Fig. 105), place them together *front-to-front,* line up the stitches to be joined, and stitch through only the outside loops of the two edges (Fig. 106).

If two sections are to be attached like those shown in Figure 107 (this is how the gusset is attached to the sides of the attaché case), stitch through both loops.

FIGURE 106

FIGURE 107

To crochet sections of crochet together, simply think of the two lined-up edges as a single row of stitches to be crocheted into. Using Slip Stitches (for a less noticeable join) or Single Crochet, crochet into all the loops in both edges or only into the outside loops.

CARRYING YARN

Concealing yarn ends isn't the only reason for carrying yarn. Sophisticated crocheters use the technique in a variety of different ways: for working two-color, back-and-forth stripe patterns that are tieless, knotless, and loose end free; for working complex designs in two-color tapestry crochet; for adding body and thickness to the crochet fabric. Carrying yarn has another use in Hard Crochet—it reinforces the crochet, making it even stronger and even more inelastic.

Yarn is always carried *behind* the row or round being crocheted; it is impossible to carry it any other way. If you crochet neatly and evenly, and if the carried yarn is kept running straight through the work, it should not be visible from either side of the crochet.

If a carried yarn is carried loosely and it doesn't run straight, something else is likely to happen. When you pull the hook back through stitches in the previous row, the hook could easily catch onto a loosely carried yarn in the row below and pull it out of the work and into view. This rarely happens to a carefully carried yarn.

To keep it running straight through the work, give an occasional tug on the carried yarn. You should feel the yarn straightening as you pull on it. Give a tug every ten or so stitches, but do it gently. Pull too hard on a carried yarn while crocheting in the round and it will pull the rim of the piece inward, acting something like the drawstring on a laundry bag. Tug too hard on a yarn carried in back-and-forth crochet and it could pull the sides in, making the work narrower. So, pull the carried yarn only enough to keep it running straight, not so much that it changes the gauge of the crochet.

CARRYING YARN FOR "ENDLESS" STRIPES

Suppose you want to use two colors of yarn to crochet something with narrow, two-row-wide, back-and-forth stripes. You could tie on new yarn for each color change, changing yarns *every two rows!* Even if you crocheted over the yarn ends with each change, all that tying and all those knots and ends would make for pretty tedious, slow-going work. What do you do?

The solution is simple: Carry the yarn that's not being worked along behind the yarn with which you're crocheting. When you reach the end of a row where a yarn change is to be made (Fig. 108; notice the carried yarn), pick up the carried yarn and yarn it through to complete the last stitch in the row (Fig. 109). Then chain, turn, place the old yarn behind the work, and crochet away, carrying the old yarn along. Don't forget to give the carried yarn a gentle tug now and then. Carry the yarn all the

FIGURE 108

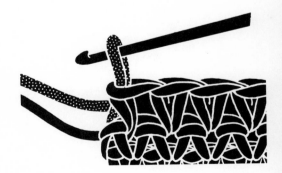

FIGURE 109

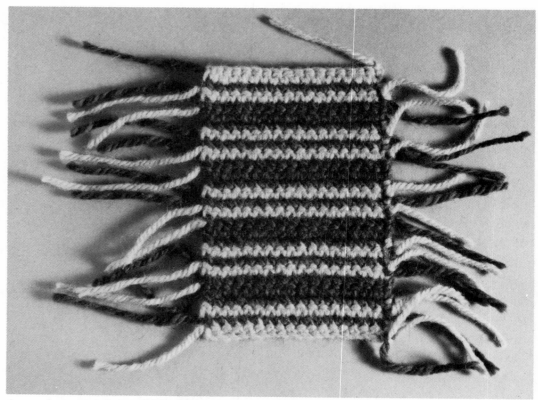

A crochet swatch in which new yarn was tied on for each change of color, resulting in numerous loose ends that will have to be worked in later.

way to the point where the next yarn change is called for. At that point, bring up the carried yarn and start carrying the other. Using this simple method, you can crochet miles of stripes with nary a knot or a single loose end.

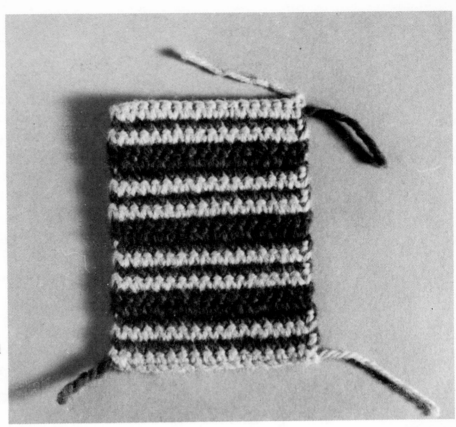

Carrying the yarn not in use behind the yarn being worked eliminates loose ends and saves lots of work later on.

CARRYING YARN FOR TWO-COLOR TAPESTRY CROCHET

The baskets on pages 89, 92, and 96 are all examples of tapestry crochet. So is the hat on page 132. All of these objects are worked in the round. The belt designs are examples of tapestry crochet worked in back-and-forth rows.

Simply defined, tapestry crochet is the working of two-color designs (other than stripes) by alternating between two yarns, one of which is worked while the other is carried. Simple stripe patterns require switching yarns only at the ends of rows. A complicated tapestry crochet design can call for a yarn change at any point in the work, possibly dozens of them in a single row or round.

Switching from one yarn to the other in the middle of a round or row is easily done. When the pattern calls for the next stitch to be worked with the yarn that's being carried, do not complete the stitch before it—stop instead just short of yarning through the last two loops on the hook (Fig. 110). Yarn the carried color over the hook and yarn it through both loops to complete the stitch (Fig. 111). Work the next stitch with the new yarn (Fig. 112). When the next change is called for, bring the carried yarn up the way it was for the last change and crochet with it, carrying the other yarn along, until the next change has to be made.

FIGURE 110

FIGURE 111

FIGURE 112

CARRYING YARN FOR ADDED BODY

Yarn is sometimes carried even when there are no loose ends to hide or yarn switching to be done. Sometimes yarn is carried just for the thickness and body it imparts to the crochet.

Make a sample swatch in which a yarn is carried throughout. Feel how much thicker the carried yarn makes the fabric. Take an earlier sample swatch and compare it with the new one.

Both the attaché case on page 141 and the tote bag on page 115 had yarn carried throughout. Most superblocked and felted Hard Crochet carries yarn for the thickness and body it gives the work. Whenever possible, the yarn carried for thickness should be the same as the yarn being crocheted; then, there's no need to worry about the carried yarn showing.

CARRYING YARN FOR EXTRA STRENGTH

Figure 113 shows how a carried yarn travels through back-and-forth crochet work. In addition to thickness, such a carried yarn adds an unbelievable amount of strength to the crochet fabric. The side panels of the attaché case have yarn running through them in this way,

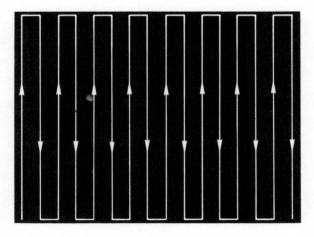

FIGURE 113

helping to reinforce the already strong and inelastic felted material. Each panel comprises 74 rows of stitches, each row having a length of inelastic yarn running tightly through it. That's a total of 148 reinforcing strands (two panels' worth) preventing the weight of the case's contents from stretching the crochet. For some idea of the strength 148 strands of three-ply acrylic carpet yarn provides, take just a half-dozen strands and try breaking them. Better still, take the sample you carried yarn through for thickness. Try to stretch it. Case closed.

IN-THE-ROUND TAPESTRY CROCHET: CREATING DESIGNS WITH A SPECIAL KIND OF GRAPH

There's nothing quite as satisfying as watching a beautifully intricate two-color tapestry crochet design develop as you crochet in the round, your nimble fingers switching back and forth between the two yarns as they respond to the demands of the pattern, working one yarn while carrying the other. But what's guiding you as you work the complicated design? How do you know exactly when and where to make the proper yarn changes? Are you looking at some kind of picture of the design as you work? A drawing? A photograph? How do you determine the number of stitches to crochet between two separate design elements? And how can you tell what the design you are crocheting is going to look like when it's finished? Will it really come out the way you picture it in your mind's eye?

Weavers follow pattern drafts that tell them how to manipulate the loom's heddles to create complex plaids and other intricate patterns. Needlepointers work on preprinted or painted canvases or follow grids covered with symbols representing the various colors in a design or picture.

In-the-round crochet designs can be plotted and graphed, as well. Using regular graph paper, two-dimensional patterns and designs can be translated into in-the-round crochet terms: into rounds and into stitches.

The graph's horizontal lines of squares can represent individual crochet rounds; each square can represent an individual stitch. On such a graph, any design can be worked out stitch-by-stitch, and, perhaps more important, can be followed stitch-by-stitch while crocheting. If every element of a design is translated into graph squares that represent every round and every stitch and you follow the graph religiously, you should have no trouble crocheting a design without having to make a single extra calculation. Sounds ideal, doesn't it? There's only one catch. A design worked out on regular graph paper does not accurately depict what the finished tapestry crochet design will look like.

A round of crochet stitches runs in a straight, horizontal line, as do the squares on graph paper. Graph squares also run straight up and down (if it's good graph paper, they do), but individual in-the-round crochet stitches don't. Instead, they run one above the other at a slight but definite angle to the horizontal (see Fig. 114). In crochet that's worked fairly tightly, the angle is around 98 degrees, enough of a slant to have a profound effect on a tapestry crochet design. Normal graph paper obviously doesn't account for this phenomenon and can therefore render only a distortion of the finished crochet design.

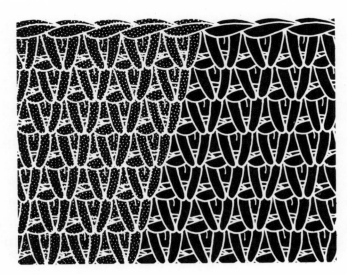

FIGURE 114

Knowing exactly what a finished design will look like before it's finished can be important. Some designs could suffer from the natural slant of the stitches; others might actually benefit from it and use the slant effect to great advantage. But if you render a design on everyday graph paper, how are you to know?

Since nobody makes in-the-round tapestry crochet graph paper with squares that run at a 98-degree slant, I had to make my own. I designed a graph that took the natural slanting of stitches into account and, for good measure, made individual stitch squares that more closely resemble real crochet stitches. The new graph worked very well; designs worked out on it translated without distortion into crochet. With this new graph paper, what I designed was what I got.

A full-size graph is reproduced on page 71. It's there for you to copy and use. Take the whole book to the nearest, or your favorite, photocopy store and have as many copies as you want made. If you anticipate using the graph often, it might be more economical to have the graph offset. Once a good supply is in hand, you will be ready to turn beautiful designs into beautiful crochet; and what you design will be what you get.

To translate any design into a crochetable graph pattern, simply work it out on the special graph sheet. A #2 pencil will give the best results. Change and alter the pattern until it conforms exactly to what you want the finished crochet to look like. Figure out the entire design, all the way around, to determine how many stitches around to make the shape the design is for.

To work a design from a graph sheet, first work the crocheted object up to the point where it contains the same number of stitches around as the design (or is the multiple of one element in a design with elements that repeat). You will then be ready to start using the graph pattern. Simply follow the graph along a stitch at a time, changing from one yarn to the other wherever the graph so indicates. If you are joining rounds, begin following the pattern at the point of the join.

Study some of the patterns worked in the book. Observe how they translate from graph to reality.

Tapestry Crochet Design Graph, ©Mark Dittrick, 1978.

A two-color design tested out in a *test tube*.

A test tube for a pattern in which the yarn being worked is switched for each and every stitch.

72

MAKING TEST TUBES

There will be times when you will want to see what a design you have created will look like in a particular yarn or how two yarns work together with respect to a design or whether a design really looks as good in yarn as it does on paper. In cases like these, it wouldn't hurt to give the yarn a tryout. The way to do that is to make a *test tube*. No, not that kind of test tube; instead a small crocheted tube in which you work the design you want to use for a basket, hat, or other object.

To make a test tube, chain just enough chains to make a tube that's just large enough to work a portion or an element of the design you want to try out. Work a few rounds, and then begin working from the design on the special graph sheet, or work from right off the top of your head. When the tube is finished, fasten off and keep it to refer to later.

Before you begin tackling original designs for major projects, you might want to first work some simple patterns on the special graph sheet and then try them out in test tubes.

LEARNING TO CROCHET THE HARD WAY

Crocheting hard isn't really very hard, but the easiest way to learn to crochet tight enough for Hard Crochet is to work up to it gradually. The following exercises were designed with that idea in mind. To work these exercises, you will need three steel hooks with homemade handles—a #00, a #0, and a #1—and a quantity of three-ply synthetic carpet yarn, or a suitable substitute.

Exercise 1: With the #00 hook and the three-ply yarn, chain 40, making the chains fairly loose. Join the ends of the chain and work around it with Single Crochet. Work six more rounds at a gauge of 4 stitches to the inch. When you have completed the sixth round, put down the #00 hook and take up the #0.

Work six more rounds with the #0 hook, increasing the gauge to 5 stitches to the inch. The tighter gauge will cause the tube to get narrower and the crochet will become noticeably stiffer. When you have finished making these six rounds, switch to the #1 hook.

Work six more rounds with the #1 hook, gradually increasing the gauge to 6 stitches to the inch. Keep a firm grip on the crochet hook and hold the developing tube tightly with the fingers of your other hand. Work slowly and methodically at first; concentrate on making each stitch exactly as tight as all the others. Don't force the hook through stitches in the round below, but find the place where it fits through easily. Work fluidly and try to develop a rhythm: Insert the hook; yarn over and through; yarn over; yarn through the loop; insert the hook; yarn over and through; yarn over; yarn through the loop; insert the hook; yarn over and through; yarn over; yarn through the loop; insert the hook; yarn over and through; yarn over; yarn through the loop; and so on. Notice that four somewhat distinct movements go into the making of each stitch. Count as you work: 1 (insert the hook), 2 (yarn over and through), 3 (yarn over), 4 (yarn through the loop), 1, 2, 3, 4; 1, 2, 3, 4; 1, 2, 3, 4; 1, 2, 3, 4.

At 6 stitches to the inch, the tube should be quite rigid and a lot narrower than it was at 4 stitches to the inch. Work a dozen more rounds at this gauge. At some point along the way, you might try crocheting even tighter to find out just how tight and rigid the particular yarn you are working with will crochet.

Make another tube, starting it with the #0 hook and a gauge of 5 stitches to the inch. After a few rounds, switch to the #1 hook and work up to 6 stitches to the inch.

Begin one more tube with the #1 hook and work it from start to finish at a gauge of 6 stitches to the inch.

Exercise 2: With the #1 hook and the three-ply carpet yarn, chain 4 loose chains and join the ends of the chain with a Slip Stitch. Working as *loosely* as you can with the #1 hook, work a few rounds in the prescribed manner for making a flat round. (Work only into the back part of loops for the first few rounds—it's easier than working under the full loop.) Stop at the end of the second no-increase round. Measure the gauge. Even though you consciously tried to crochet loosely, you probably found yourself working at a gauge somewhere between 4 and 4.5 stitches to the inch.

Make another flat round with the same yarn and hook. This time, do not consciously try to work loosely. After working the second even round, check the gauge. It's quite possible that the #1 hook's natural tendency to make small stitches will have increased the gauge to somewhere between 5 to 5.5 stitches to the inch.

Make one more flat round with the same yarn and hook. This time, though, make the stitches as tight as you can. Hold the hook firmly and keep a tight grip on the developing flat round as you work. Don't try to work too quickly and don't force the hook through the stitches or wrench the yarn back through. Easy, methodical, fluid motions are the key to making even and uniformly rigid stitches.

Exercise 3: Using the #00 hook again and the three-ply carpet yarn, chain 21. Work a fairly loose row of Single Crochet back over the chain. Turn the work and crochet about six more rows at a gauge of 4 stitches to the inch. When the last of these rows is done, change to a smaller hook.

With the #0 hook, work six more rows at a gauge of 5 stitches to the inch. When all six rows have been worked, switch to the #1 hook and crochet six more rows at a gauge of 6 stitches to the inch. The crochet should have gotten narrower and stiffer with each hook change.

Make another swatch like the first, but keep the crochet from narrowing by working in the following manner: Make five evenly spaced increases in the row in which the gauge went from 4 stitches to the inch to 5 stitches to the inch; make five more evenly spaced increases in the row in which the gauge was increased to 6 stitches to the inch. Each of these increased rows will compensate for the greater tightness of the stitches worked at the higher gauge; the crochet should remain five inches wide. Try it.

Make one more swatch. Start this time with the #1 hook and begin crocheting at 6 stitches to the inch. Start by making small chains, and work into the chain with carefully made and tightly worked stitches. Work additional rows at the same gauge. Working this way may be a bit difficult at first, but it should get easier with a little practice.

Superblocking

Superblocking—a hot iron plus lots of steam and lots of pressure—turns not very spectacular, tightly worked, back-and-forth crochet into superstrong and inelastic felted Hard Crochet. Crochet a fairly large swatch (six inches by six inches will be sufficient) with the three-ply carpet yarn at a gauge of between 5.5 and 6 stitches to the inch; then, follow this series of simple steps:

Step 1: Find a hard, stable, and suitably flat surface to work on—an ordinary ironing board won't do. You may want to lay down a few sheets of newspaper to protect the surface.

Step 2: Lay the crochet down on the surface (Fig. 115).

Step 3: Place a thin cotton towel over the crochet (Fig. 116).

Step 4: Spray the towel with a generous amount of water (Fig. 117); let it soak through to the crochet.

Step 5: Place a hot iron—it should be set on the "linen" setting—down on the towel (Fig. 118).

Step 6: Applying considerable downward pressure, iron back and forth vigorously (Fig. 119).

Step 7: Remove the iron (Fig. 120).

Step 8: Remove the towel (Fig. 121). Notice how flat the crochet got. The swatch should still be steaming.

Step 9: Allow the crochet to cool; as it does, it will gradually plump up to its original thickness (Fig. 122).

FIGURE 115

FIGURE 116

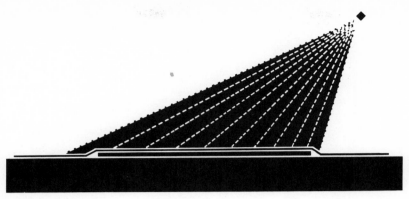

FIGURE 117

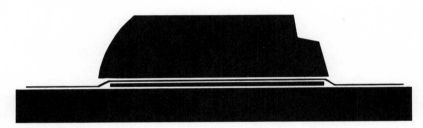

FIGURE 118

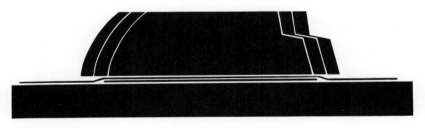

FIGURE 119

FIGURE 120

FIGURE 121

FIGURE 122

MAKING THINGS THE HARD WAY

Hints, Suggestions, Reminders

Here are just a few thoughts to make crocheting hard a little bit easier:

When carrying yarn, don't forget to give an occasional tug on the carried yarn to keep it running straight through the work.

Check every so often to make sure you haven't accidentally dropped or added any stitches when working a long series of rounds or rows.

Measure your work occasionally to make sure the desired dimensions are being properly maintained.

Remember that to *work even* in a round or row means to not increase or decrease.

Work all stitches with easy, fluid motions. If crocheting becomes difficult, it's probably because you're trying to crochet hard too hard. A bent crochet hook head will also make working very difficult. Check the head of your hook occasionally for signs of bending due to long periods of working hard. Discard bent hooks and replace them with new ones.

Yarn wound in a ball for more convenient use.

Roll yarn into medium-size balls for easier working, and keep loose yarn ends fastened to the balls when not in use to avoid tangles.

Make sure you have enough of the yarn called for before beginning a project.

After working the first few rounds or rows of a piece, check to see if you're crocheting at the correct gauge.

If a design or pattern looks a bit difficult or you aren't sure if a yarn is suitable for a particular project, make a test swatch or test tube before starting the actual piece.

Whenever possible, work in loose yarn ends as you crochet.

Belts

Since they are little more than long, narrow strips worked in short, back-and-forth rows (Fig. 123), few things are easier to crochet than belts. Five belts are shown here: two with their buckles—one having grommets set into the material and the other with a simple border design; and three details from belts worked in fancy, back-and-forth tapestry crochet.

The belt with the grommets is simply a long, 7-stitch-wide strip (gauge: 6 stitches to the inch) with holes left in the material (the result of chaining and skipping the middle stitch in the previous row) every eighth row. Grommets are set into the holes with a simple grommet setter. At the fastening end of the belt, grommets are set in every fourth row. A row of Single Crochet borders the belt, and the buckle is simply laced to the starting-chain end of the strip. When it's finished, the entire belt, grommets and all, is superblocked.

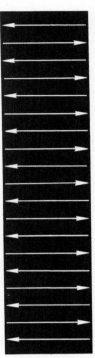

FIGURE 123

Using a tapestry needle and a length of yarn, belt end and buckle are easily lashed together.

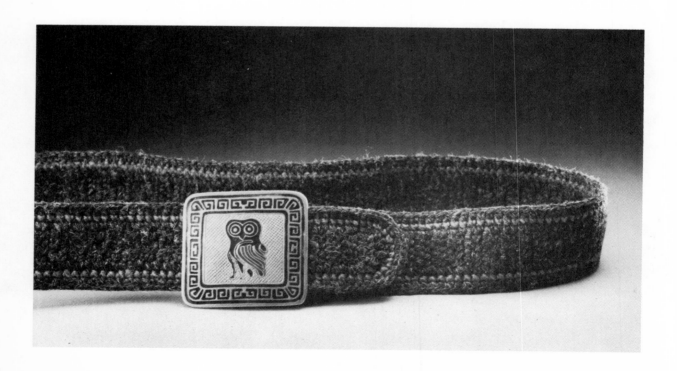

The belt with the owl on its buckle is even easier to make; it's nothing more than a long, 4-stitch-wide strip (gauge: 6 stitches to the inch again) with three bordering rows—two in the color of the belt and one row between them in a contrasting color.

Because they are so easy to make, belt strips are perfect vehicles for complex, two-color crochet patterns. The three designs shown and explained here call for numerous yarn changes, the first being perhaps the ultimate tapestry pattern, requiring a switch for every stitch.

Belt 1

TAPESTRY BELT PATTERN 1

Chain 10 with the lighter yarn A.

Row 1: Work a row of Singles back over the chain, chain and turn. Begin carrying the darker yarn B at the beginning of the row.

Row 2: Work an incomplete Single; bring up B to complete the stitch, and work an incomplete Single; switch to A; switch to B; switch to A; switch to B; switch to A; switch to B; switch to A; bring up B, chain and turn.

Row 3: Work an incomplete Single; switch to A; switch to B; switch to A; switch to B; switch to A; switch to B; switch to A; switch to B; bring up A, chain and turn.

Row 4: Repeat Row 2.

Row 5: Repeat Row 3.

Row 6: Repeat Row 2.

Row 7: Repeat Row 3.

And so forth.

Belt 2

TAPESTRY BELT PATTERN 2

Chain 9 with the lighter yarn A.

Row 1: Work Singles back over the chain, chain and turn. Begin carrying the darker yarn B at the beginning of the row.

Row 2: Work 3 Singles and an incomplete Single; bring up B to complete the Single and work 4 Singles, chain and turn.

Row 3: Work 3 Singles and an incomplete Single; bring up A and work 3 Singles and an incomplete Single; bring up B, chain and turn.

Row 4: Work 3 Singles and an incomplete Single; bring up A and work 4 Singles, chain and turn.

Row 5: Work 3 Singles and an incomplete Single; bring up B and work 3 Singles and an incomplete Single; bring up A, chain and turn.

Row 6: Repeat Row 2.

Row 7: Repeat Row 3.

Row 8: Repeat Row 4.

Row 9: Repeat Row 5.

Row 10: Repeat Row 2.

And so on.

TAPESTRY BELT PATTERN 3

Chain 11 with the lighter yarn A; carrying yarn B, work a row of Singles back over the chain, chain and turn. Switching between the two yarns, work rows according to the following plan, reading from the bottom up:

```
              A A A B B A A B B A ←——
    ——→ A A B B A A B B A A
              A A A B B A A B B A ←——
    ——→ A A B B A A B B A A
              A A A B B A A B B A ←——
    ——→ A A B B A A B B A A
              A A A B B A A B B A ←——
```

Baskets

Rather than give each of the following baskets a silly, descriptive name, I've chosen to number them; it's easier for me and less embarrassing for the baskets.

BASKET 1

The design in this basket requires numerous yarn changes to achieve a dramatic optical pattern, a pattern that uses the natural slant of stitches worked in the round to great advantage.

In addition to the pattern graph provided for the basket shown here, a variation for a taller basket is given. You might want to alter the pattern even further to see what other interesting designs you can devise.

Dimensions: 3½ inches high by 5 inches wide.
Yarn: Two colors of three-ply acrylic/modacrylic carpet yarn or suitable substitutes—approximately 5 ounces of the lighter color and a small quantity of the darker color.
Hook: Steel #1.
Gauge: 6.5 stitches = 1 inch.

With the lighter-color yarn, chain 4 and connect the ends of the chain with a Slip Stitch.

Rounds 1 through 3: Increase in every stitch around until there are 26 stitches around.

Round 4: Work even. Begin joining rounds.

Round 5: Increase in every other stitch—39 stitches around.

Round 6: Work even.

Round 7: Increase in every 3rd stitch—52 stitches around.

Round 8: Work even.

Basket 1

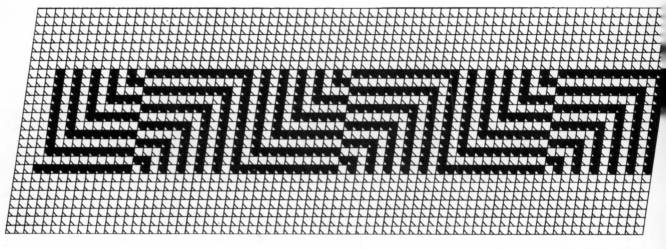

Design graph, Basket 1

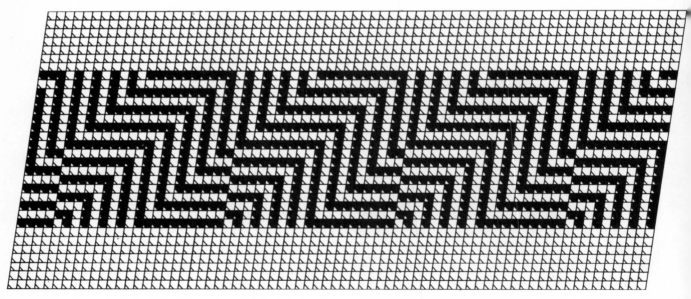

A variation

Round 9: Increase in every 4th stitch—65 stitches around.

Round 10: Work even.

Round 11: Increase in every 5th stitch—78 stitches around.

Round 12: Work even.

Round 13: Increase in every 6th stitch—91 stitches around.

Round 14: Work even.

Round 15: Increase in every 7th stitch—104 stitches around.

Round 16: Work even.

Round 17: Increase in every 10th stitch—114 stitches around.

Rounds 18 and 19: Work even. In the middle of Round 19, start carrying the darker yarn.

Rounds 20 through 29: After joining rounds, begin following the pattern graph.

Rounds 30 and 31: In the middle of Round 30, stop carrying the darker yarn.

Round. 32: *Decrease* every 10 stitches—104 stitches around.

Round 33: Work even. Join, fasten off, and carefully work in the loose yarn end.

BASKET 2

This design, a quasi-American Indian motif that was improvised on a sheet of the special design graph paper, might be thought of as a series of big teeth pointing downward with more numerous smaller teeth running around above.

The design on the bottom of the basket echoes the larger design, but here the teeth look more like the petals of a flower. This bottom pattern cannot be easily graphed because of the many increases; round-by-round instructions are therefore given for working this part of the basket's design.

The tip of each downward-pointing tooth is an increase, represented on the design graph here by the elimi-

Basket 2

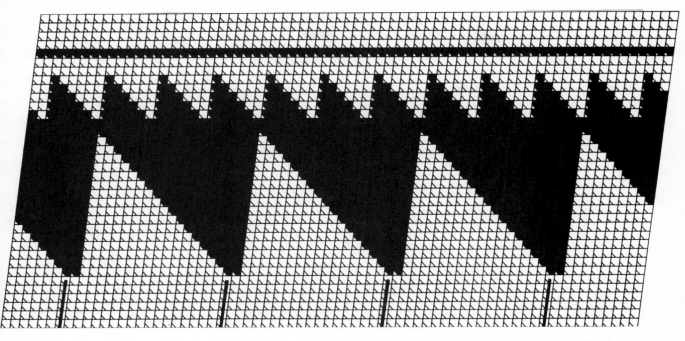

Design graph, Basket 2

A flower petallike design covers the bottom of the basket.

nation of a vertical line of stitches below the increase. Perhaps you can come up with a better way to indicate increases on a pattern graph.

Dimensions: 6 inches high by 5½ inches wide.
Yarn: Two colors of three-ply acrylic/modacrylic carpet yarn or suitable substitutes—about 4 ounces of yarn A and 4 ounces of yarn B.
Hook: Steel #1.
Gauge: 7 stitches = inch.

With yarn A, chain 4 and connect the ends of the chain with a Slip Stitch.

Rounds 1 through 3: increase in each stitch around until there are 28 stitches around.

Round 4: Work even. Begin carrying yarn B. Do not join rounds, but keep track of where new rounds begin and end.

Round 5: Increase in every other stitch—42 stitches around.

Round 6: Work even.

Round 7: Increase in every 3rd stitch—56 stitches around.

Round 8: Work even.

Round 9: Increase in every 4th stitch—70 stitches around.

Round 10: Work even.

Round 11: Increase in every 5th stitch—84 stitches around. For the 1st increase in the round, bring up yarn B and use it to make only the 2 stitches of the increase; switch back to yarn A and make the next 4 Singles, then increase in the 5th stitch, and the next 4 Singles; bring up yarn B to work the 2 stitches of the increase; switch back to yarn A and continue around, switching to yarn B for working every other increase.

Round 12: Work even. Bring up yarn B to work into the 2 stitches of each yarn-B increase in the previous round *and* into the stitch immediately following the increase; switch back to yarn A after each group of 3 yarn-B stitches.

Round 13: Increase in every 12th stitch—91 stitches around. For this and following rounds until otherwise instructed, continue switching between yarn A and yarn B as for Round 12, and make all increases in the yarn-B section of each round.

Round 14: Work even.

Round 15: Increase in every 13th stitch—98 stitches around.

Round 16: Work even.

Round 17: Increase in every 14th stitch—105 stitches around.

Round 18: Work even.

Round 19: Increase in every 15th stitch—112 stitches around.

Round 20: Work even. The final yarn-A stitches in this section of the basket will be worked in this round.

Round 21: Increase in every 16th stitch—119 stitches around.

Round 22: Work even.

Rounds 23 through 48: Increase in every 17th stitch—126 stitches around. Bring up yarn A to work the 2 stitches of each increase; switch back to yarn B for all other stitches in the round. Begin following the pattern graph. Join the last 3 rounds. At the end of Round 48, join, fasten off, and carefully work in the fastened-off end.

BASKET 3

The first design graph is the one that was used for crocheting the basket shown here; it very closely duplicates a design on a cooking basket the Yurok Indians of northern California used to make acorn mush. The recipe for the mush may have been lost over the years, but thank goodness the basket and its design survive.

The other two design graphs, selected from quite a few others that were made, are variations on the original design and serve to illustrate how one design can easily be manipulated to create many more.

Basket 3

Design graph, Basket 3

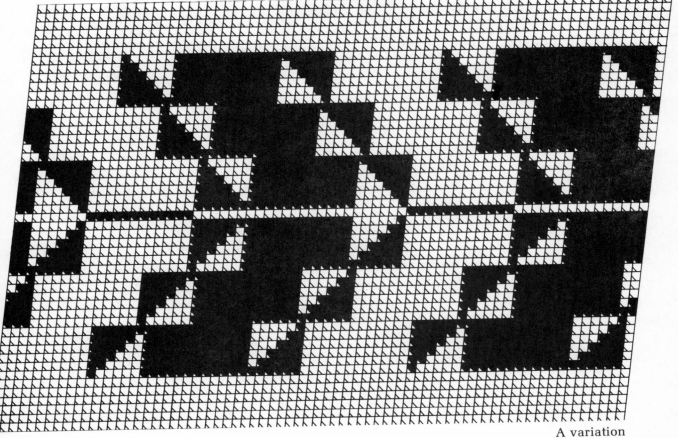

A variation

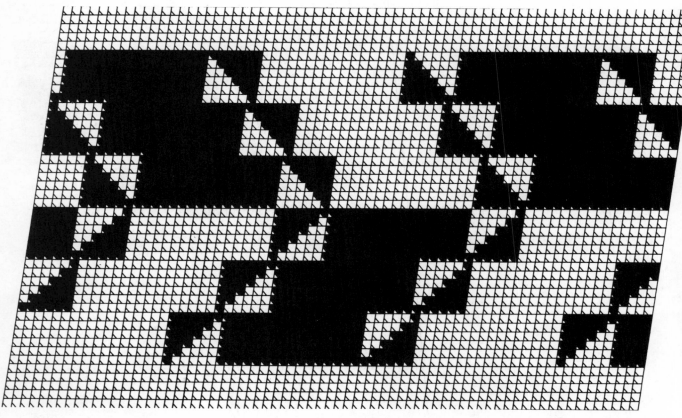

Another variation

Like the basket on page 107, this one also has a shaped bottom and is worked in the same unusually tight-crocheting yarn from The Weaver's Store in Boston.

Dimensions: 6 inches high by 6 inches wide.
Yarn: Approximately 4 ounces each of two colors of synthetic yarn.
Hook: Steel #1.
Gauge: 6.75 stitches = 1 inch.

With the light-colored yarn, chain 4 and connect the ends of the chain with a Slip Stitch.

Rounds 1 through 3: Increase in every stitch around until there are 24 stitches around.

Round 4: Work even. Begin joining rounds.

Round 5: Increase in every other stitch—36 stitches around.

Round 6: Work even.

Round 7: Increase in every 3rd stitch—48 stitches around.

Round 8: Work even.

Round 9: Increase in every 4th stitch—60 stitches around.

Round 10: Work even.

Round 11: Increase in every 5th stitch—72 stitches around.

Round 12: Work even.

Round 13: Increase in every 6th stitch—84 stitches around.

Rounds 14 through 19: Work even.

Round 20: Increase in every 8th stitch—95 stitches around.

Round 21: Work even. Push the bottom in, and mold it into a contoured bottom by pushing the center back out.

Round 22: Increase in every 9th stitch—106 stitches around.

Round 23: Work even.

Round 24: Increase in every 10th stitch—117 stitches around.

Round 25: Work even.

Round 26: Increase in every 11th stitch—128 stitches around.

Rounds 27 and 28: Work even.

Round 29: Increase in every 32nd stitch—132 stitches around.

The shape of the basket's bottom illustrates Hard Crochet's amazing malleability.

Rounds 30 and 31: Work even. In the middle of Round 31, begin carrying the darker yarn.

Rounds 32 through 55: Follow the design graph, working three complete light areas between three complete dark elements. At the end of Round 55, fasten off and carefully work in the fastened-off end.

BASKET 4

I couldn't resist giving this basket a name; I call it the *little dashes* basket.

The design for which the basket is named looks something like a technique known as woven crochet, but it

Basket 4

A test tube was first made to figure out the "little dashes" basket's intricate design.

isn't. In woven crochet, yarn is sewn through a piece after the crocheting is done. The little dashes in this basket, however, are created by alternately exposing and concealing a carried yarn. Requiring some fairly intricate finger manipulation, this technique is a lot of fun to work once the knack of it is gotten, and the results are well worth the effort.

Dimensions: 3 inches by 4 inches wide.

Yarn: Two contrasting colors of three-ply acrylic/mod-acrylic carpet yarn, or suitable substitutes—about 2 ounces of yarn A and about an ounce of yarn B.

Hook: Steel #1.

Gauge: Just over 6 stitches = 1 inch.

With yarn A, chain 4 and connect the ends of the chain with a Slip Stitch.

Rounds 1 through 3: Increase in every stitch around until there are 26 stitches around.

Round 4: Work even. Begin joining rounds.

Round 5: Increase in every other stitch—39 stitches around.

Round 6: Work even.

Round 7: Increase in every 3rd stitch—52 stitches around.

Round 8: Work even.

Round 9: Increase in every 4th stitch—65 stitches around.

Round 10: Work even.

Round 11: Increase in every 5th stitch—78 stitches around.

Round 12: Work even.

Round 13: Increase in every 10th stitch—86 stitches around.

Round 14: Work even. Begin carrying yarn B.

Round 15: Bring up yarn B and carry yarn A.

Round 16: Alternate between carrying A and exposing it: Bring A out from behind the stitches and toward you; make a Single in the next stitch with B; return A to the carrying position behind the round of stitches and work a Single over it with B; bring A out and toward you again; work another Single with B; return A to the carrying position and work over it with B. Continue working in this manner all the way around.

Round 17: Carry A all the way around.

Round 18: Bring up A and carry B.

Round 19: After the join, work 18 stitches with A, alternating between carrying and exposing B; bring up B and work 14 stitches, carrying A all the way; bring up A and work 16 stitches, alternately carrying and exposing B; bring up B and carry A for 14 stitches; bring up A and work 12 stitches, alternately carrying and exposing B; bring up B and carry A for 12 stitches; join rounds while switching to A.

Round 20: Work A as far as you worked it in the previous round, alternately carrying and exposing B—this time, shift the exposed yarn 1 space so the little dashes *do not* line up above the little dashes in the round below. Bring up B and work 14 stitches, alternately carrying and exposing A; bring up A and work 16 stitches, alternating between exposing and carrying B and shifting the little dashes as before. Continue around in this fashion.

Rounds 21 through 25: Work around as for Round 20, always shifting dashes so they do not line up with dashes in the previous round. In Round 25, carry A without exposing it.

Round 26: Work around with B, carrying A.

Rounds 27, 28, and 29: Work as for Rounds 15, 16, and 17. Fasten off and carefully work in the fastened-off yarn end.

BASKET 5

This basket owes its incredible strength (see the demonstration on page 18) to the extreme tightness of its stitches and the unusual nature of the synthetic yarn used to crochet it. Not an acrylic/modacrylic carpet yarn from The Mannings, but a strange synthetic from The Weaver's Store in Boston, this yarn crochets at a very high gauge with very little effort.

Dimensions: 8 inches high by 6 inches wide.
Yarn: Approximately 8 ounces of the yarn mentioned in the description.
Hook: Steel #1.
Gauge: 7 stitches = 1 inch.

Chain 4 and connect the ends of the chain with a Slip Stitch.

Rounds 1 through 3: Increase into each stitch around until there are 28 stitches around.

Round 4: Work even. Begin joining rounds.

Basket 5

Round 5: Increase in every other stitch—42 stitches around.

Round 6: Work even.

Round 7: Increase in every 7th stitch—48 stitches around.

Round 8: Increase in every 4th stitch—60 stitches around.

Rounds 9, 10, and 11: Work even.

Round 12: Increase in every 6th stitch—70 stitches around.

Round 13: Work even.

Round 14: Increase in every 6th stitch—82 stitches around.

Round 15: Work even.

Round 16: Alternate between increasing in every 7th stitch and every 8th stitch in the round—93 stitches around.

Round 17: Work even.

Round 18: Alternate between increasing in every 8th stitch and every 9th stitch in the round—104 stitches around.

Rounds 19 and 20: Work even.

Round 21: Increase in every 34th stitch—107 stitches around.

Round 22: Work even.

Round 23: Increase in every 35th stitch—110 stitches around.

Round 24: Work even. Make a contoured bottom by pushing the bottom in and then pushing its center back out.

Round 25: Increase in every 36th stitch—113 stitches around.

Round 26: Work even.

Round 27: Increase in every 37th stitch—116 stitches around.

Round 28: Work even.

Round 29: Increase in every 38th stitch—119 stitches around.

Round 30: Work even.

Round 31: Increase in every 39th stitch—122 stitches around.

The basket bottom is shaped like the bottom of Basket 3.

Round 32: Work even.

Round 33: Increase in every 40th stitch—125 stitches around.

Rounds 34 through 37: Work even.

Round 38: *Decrease* every 20 stitches—119 stitches around.

Round 39: Work even.

Round 40: Decrease every 19 stitches—113 stitches around.

Round 41: Work even.

Round 42: Decrease every 18 stitches—107 stitches around.

Round 43: Work even.

Round 44: Decrease every 17 stitches—101 stitches around.

Round 45: Work even.

Round 46: Decrease every 16 stitches—95 stitches around.

Round 47: Work even.

Round 48: Decrease every 15 stitches—89 stitches around.

Rounds 49 through 69: Work even.

Round 70: *Increase* in every 15th stitch—95 stitches around.

Round 71: Work even.

Round 72: Increase in every 16th stitch—101 stitches around.

Rounds 73 and 74: Work even.

Round 75: Increase in every 33rd stitch—104 stitches around.

Rounds 76 and 77: Work even. Join, fasten off, and carefully work in the fastened-off yarn end.

BASKET 6

Even though I crocheted this basket, three other people had a lot to do with its design: Dutch artist M. C. Escher (1898–1972) was famous for graphic works in which the foreground and background were often interchangeable; former Peace Corps volunteer John Ortman stayed on in Quito, Ecuador, to open a shop and start an exporting business; Dan Storper owns Putumayo Imports, a shop/gallery on New York's Lexington Avenue where he deals exclusively in "handicrafts from the Andes to the Amazon." Ortman showed a reproduction of a typically eye-boggling Escher drawing, *symmetry drawing B,* to a group of native weavers. I saw the woven version at Putumayo and translated the unusual bird motif into crochet stitches on a special graph sheet. The result of all our ef-

Basket 6

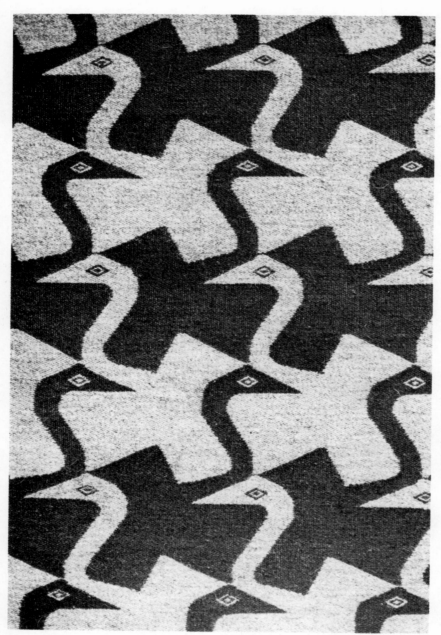

A detail of the Ecuadorean weaving that inspired the basket design. PHOTO BY THE AUTHOR.

forts is a basket with a pattern that's a design from a design from a design.

The first design graph here shows the rendered design. In the second graph, the one to follow to make the basket, the right portion of the pattern has been shifted up one space so the design can be worked without joining rounds. The first pattern stitch, the point where the first design round begins, is indicated by the arrow on the graph.

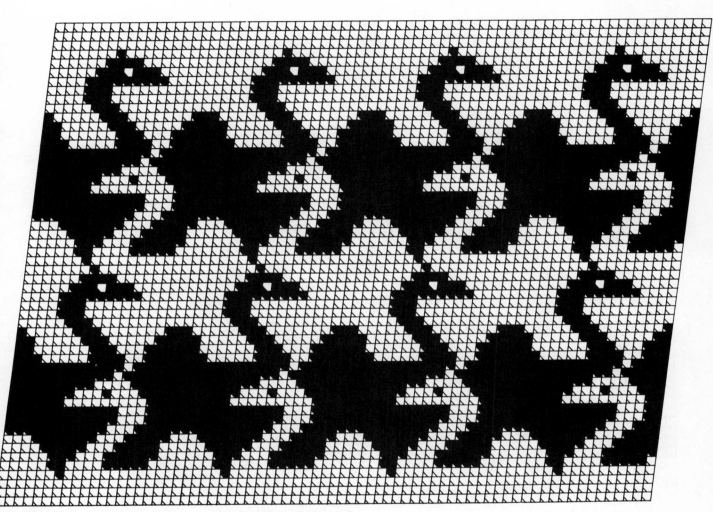

The first design graph for Basket 6. Don't follow this graph.

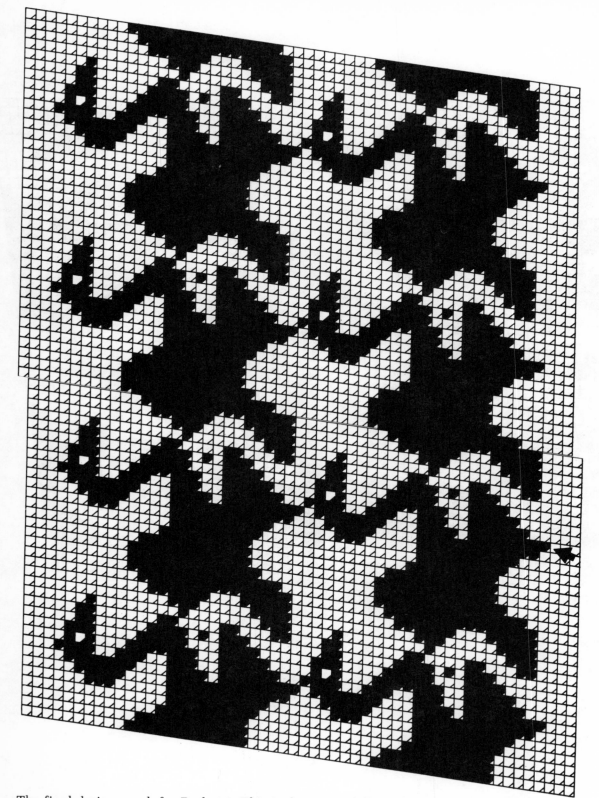

The final design graph for Basket 6. This is the one to follow, starting at the stitch indicated by the arrow.

112

Dimensions: 11 inches high by 8 inches wide.

Yarn: 1½ pounds each of two colors—one light and one dark—of three-ply acrylic/modacrylic carpet yarn or suitable substitutes.

Gauge: 6.5 stitches = 1 inch.

Hook: Steel #1.

With the light yarn, chain 3 and join the ends of the chain with a Slip Stitch.

Rounds 1 through 3: Increase in every stitch until there are 39 stitches around.

Round 4: Work even.

Round 5: Increase in every other stitch—52 stitches around.

Round 6: Work even.

Round 7: Increase in every 3rd stitch—65 stitches around.

Round 8: Work even.

Round 9: Increase in every 4th stitch—78 stitches around.

Round 10: Work even.

Round 11: Increase in every 5th stitch—91 stitches around.

Round 12: Work even.

Round 13: Increase in every 6th stitch—104 stitches around.

Round 14: Work even.

Round 15: Increase in every 7th stitch—117 stitches around.

Round 16: Work even.

Round 17: Increase in every 8th stitch—130 stitches around.

Round 18: Work even.

Round 19: Increase in every 9th stitch—143 stitches around.

Round 20: Work even.

Round 21: Increase in every 10th stitch—156 stitches around.

Round 22: Work even.

Round 23: Increase in every 17th stitch—165 stitches around.

Round 24: Work even.

Round 25: Increase in every 21st stitch—173 stitches around.

Round 26: Work even.

Round 27: Increase in every 25th stitch—180 stitches around.

Rounds 28 and 29: Work even.

Rounds 30 through 77: Begin following the pattern graph. Work even.

Rounds 78 through 81: Work even. At the end of Round 78, begin joining rounds. At the end of Round 81, join the ends of the round, fasten off, and carefully work in the loose yarn end.

Tote Bag

Fabric that's been crocheted hard and then super-blocked can take the place of heavy canvas and similar materials, as the tote bag shown here convincingly proves.

The body of the tote is made by crocheting into and away from previously crocheted sections until there is one large, flat, crosslike section (Fig. 124). Straps are attached to the body and then the extending sections are stitched together to form a tote bag that's as practical as it is pleasant to look at.

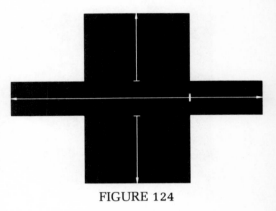

FIGURE 124

Dimensions: 9 inches high by 13 inches long by 4¼ inches wide with 17-inch-long straps.

Yarn: Four colors of three-ply acrylic/modacrylic carpet yarn or suitable substitutes—a pound and a half of A and small quantities of B, C, and D.

Hook: Steel #0.

Gauge: horizontal—5.5 stitches = 1 inch; row—4.75 rows = 1 inch.

A close-up shows how the stripe design is repeated at the base of each of the tote's straps.

Elements of the stripe motif line up perfectly at the point where the sides of the tote are stitched together.

BODY:

Chain 24 with yarn A.

Row 1: Work Singles back over the chain, working into the back of the chain for a finished chain edge—23 stitches across.

Rows 2 through 17: Begin carrying a long length of yarn A and work even rows. In the middle of Row 17, stop carrying yarn A and begin carrying yarn B.

Rows 18 and 19: Bring up B and begin carrying A. In the middle of Row 19, stop carrying A and start carrying yarn C.

Rows 20 and 21: Bring up C and carry B. In the middle of Row 21, stop carrying B and begin carrying yarn D.

Rows 22 and 23: Bring up D and carry C.

Rows 24 and 25: Bring up C and carry D. In the middle of Row 25, stop carrying D and begin carrying B.

Rows 26 and 27: Bring up B and carry C. In the middle of Row 27, stop carrying C and start carrying A again.

Rows 28 through 44: Bring up A and carry B to the middle of the row; there, stop carrying B and begin carrying a long length of A. Work even rows through Row 44; fasten off and clip the carried yarn.

Note: Notice that the stripe design does not look the same on both sides. The front, or "right side," of this fabric is the side in which the *back* of the first row of each new stripe is *facing* you.

Holding the piece so that its front is facing *away* from you, begin crocheting into the chain edge.

Rows 1 through 84: Work Singles into the chain with yarn A and work even rows through Row 84, carrying a very long length of yarn A throughout. In the middle of Row 84, stop carrying A and begin carrying B.

Rows 85 through 94: Work the B–C–D–C–B stripe pattern.

Rows 95 through 111: Bring up A; carry B to the middle of the row; stop carrying B and begin carrying a long length of A. Work to the end of Row 111, fasten off, and clip the carried yarn.

With the front of the fabric facing you, find the exact middle of one of the long, raw edges—the shape is 157 rows long, so Row 79 (counting from either end) should mark the middle of the piece. Mark the middle point along the edge with a small piece of yarn. Count 33 spaces (rows) to the right of the middle marker (don't count the marked space) and mark that space. Count 33 spaces (rows) to the left of the middle marker and mark that space. Tie yarn A to the side of the right-hand marker.

Row 1: Work a Single in the marked space and work a bordering row along the edge, *increasing into every 6th stitch space*, until you reach and complete a stitch in the space indicated by the left-hand marker—78 stitches across. Chain and turn.

Rows 2 through 19: Begin carrying a long length of yarn A and work even rows through Row 19. In the middle of Row 19, stop carrying A and start carrying B.

Rows 20 through 29: Work the B–C–D–C–B stripe pattern.

Rows 30 through 46: Bring up A; carry B to the middle of the row; stop carrying B, and begin carrying a long length of A. Work to the end of Row 46, fasten off, and clip the carried yarn.

With the front of the fabric facing you, work away from the other raw edge exactly as previously instructed. With a hot iron and a wet covering cloth, superblock the entire piece.

STRAPS:

Chain 9 with yarn A.

Row 1: Work Singles back over the chain, carrying a length of B as you work into it—8 stitches across.

Rows 2 through 11: Work the B–C–D–C–B stripe pattern.

Rows 12 through 71: Bring up A; carry B to the middle of Row 13; stop carrying B and begin carrying a long length of A. Work even rows to the end of Row 71, fasten off and clip the carried yarn.

Make three more identical strap sections. Stitch the top ends of the strap sections together to make two long straps, making sure that the fronts of the sections are facing the same way before stitching. Superblock both straps. Stitch the strap ends securely to the top edges of the wide side panels, leaving a 5½-inch space between them.

Border the entire piece, working around the edges of all four panels and around the outside part of each strap. Border the inside parts of the straps and the edge between the straps. Don't forget to increase in every sixth stitch when bordering the raw edges.

With a blunt-nosed needle threaded with long lengths of yarn A, stitch the panel edges together to form the body of the tote bag.

A Very Hard Heart

Here is a hard heart if ever there was one, and it's a heavy heart, too. Worked in two sections (a front one and a back), stitched almost together, and then stuffed until there isn't room for one more shred of stuffing, this piece is more a small, whimsical sculpture than anything else. I suppose you could also think of it as a petrified pillow.

Whatever it is, it is extremely easy to crochet; the stuffing is the real work.

Dimensions: 7 inches high by 6 inches wide by 4 inches thick.

Yarn: Small quantities of five different colors of any tough, hard, three-ply yarn (even naturals will do)—yarn A, which should be red, and four other colors (B, C, D, and E) of your choice.

Hook: Steel #0.

Gauge: 5.5 stitches = 1 inch.

Additional Materials: Lots of shredded foam or other stuffing material.

FRONT PART OF THE HEART:

With yarn A, chain 16.

Row 1: Work a row of Single Crochet back over the chain, working into the back of the chain for a finished chain edge.

Rows 2 through 15: Decrease 1 stitch in each row. "Row" 15 should be 1 stitch wide. Fasten off.

Turn the work to crochet into the chain edge. Tie on yarn A just to the left of the chain's center so that you can work into the 8 left-hand chains.

Row 1: Decrease into the 1st and last stitches in the chain and turn.

Row 2: Decrease in the 1st and last stitches in the row.

Row 3: Decrease in the 1st and last stitches in the row and fasten off.

Work into the other 8 chains the same way.

Border the heart shape with a row of yarn A, working 4 evenly spaced increases around each of the heart's upper lobes, a double increase at the bottom point and a *double decrease* (insert the hook into the next stitch; yarn over and yarn through the stitch; insert the hook into the next stitch; yarn over and yarn through the stitch; insert the hook into the next stitch; yarn over and yarn through the stitch; yarn over and yarn through all *four* loops on the hook) in the cleft at the top of the heart. Join and fasten off.

Tie on yarn B and border the heart, increasing, double increasing, and double decreasing in the appropriate places. Tie on C, border and fasten off; tie on D, border twice and fasten off; tie on C, border and fasten off; tie on B, border and fasten off; tie on C, border and fasten off; tie on D, border twice and fasten off; tie on C, border and fasten off; tie on B, border and fasten off. You should have increased, double increased, and double decreased in all of the just mentioned bordering rows. All the double decreases should have created a noticeable dimple between the two lobes of the heart.

BACK OF THE HEART:

With yarn E, chain 34.

Row 1: Work a row of Singles back over the chain, working into the back of the chain for a finished chain edge.

Rows 2 through 28: Decrease 1 stitch in each row. Turn the entire piece around and work into the chain edge.

Rows 1 through 10: Decrease 1 stitch in each row.

Border with two or three rows of Single Crochet. *Do not* work any increases.

There should be approximately the same number of stitches around the edges of both the front and back parts of the heart. If there is any difference, work one more row around the back section and either decrease or increase.

Thread a blunt-nosed needle with yarn B, and lace the front and back of the heart together, leaving a 2-inch opening at the bottom of the heart.

Through the opening, cram as much stuffing material into the heart as you possibly can. Lace up the opening.

FIGURE 125

FIGURE 126

FIGURE 127

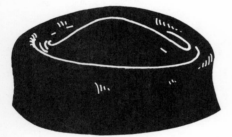
FIGURE 128

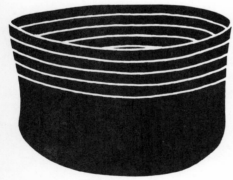
FIGURE 129

Hats

HAT 1

This hat has been the object of a strange and recurring criticism: It doesn't look handmade, or handmade enough—it's too even and regular in its shape, and it doesn't even look crocheted. It's interesting that what some see as a fault in this hat, I find to be its second greatest virtue. What most impresses me about it is its deceptive simplicity. While it may at first look complicated, with its molded crown and shaped brim, its truly simple construction becomes apparent with the few easy steps that follow.

The hat seen here was made in the following fashion:

1. A simple flat round was made (Fig. 125).
2. Following a predetermined increase pattern, the flat round was turned into a shallow dome shape (Fig. 126).
3. The dome was made deeper (Fig. 127).
4. The top of the dome was pushed in and molded into the desired shape (Fig. 128).
5. Following the increase pattern, the crown was worked down to the bottom, sometimes with a design worked into the base (Fig. 129).
6. The first brim round was worked into the *outside loops* of the bottom crown round.
7. Alternating even and increase rounds, the brim was worked out and away from the hat (Fig. 130).

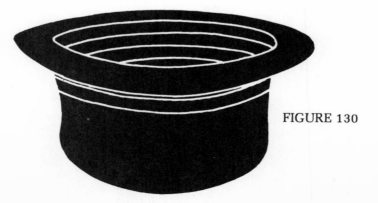
FIGURE 130

124

Hat 1

To figure out how many stitches around to make the bottom rounds of a hat crown for a particular head, follow this simple formula: Multiply the gauge by 1 more than the number of inches around the wearer's head. For example, if the gauge is 6 stitches to the inch and the head it is intended for measures 23 inches around, multiply 6 by 24 to get the number of stitches at the base of the crown—144.

If you know only the wearer's hat size, use the following to convert the size into inches around:

Head Size	Hat Size
20	6½
20½	6⅝
21	6¾
21½	6⅞
22	7
22½	7⅛
23	7¼
23½	7⅜
24	7½

Dimensions: Crown—4 inches high by 22 inches around at the base (hat size: 7); brim—2½ inches wide.

Yarn: Three colors of three-ply acrylic/modacrylic carpet yarn or suitable substitutes—approximately 9 ounces of yarn A and small quantities of yarns B and C.

Hook: Steel #1.

Gauge: 6.5 stitches = 1 inch.

Additional Materials: ¾ yard of 1½" hem facing in the color of your choice.

CROWN:

With yarn A, chain 4 and connect the ends of the chain with a Slip Stitch.

Rounds 1 through 3: Increase in each stitch around until there are 24 stitches around.

Round 4: Work even.

Round 5: Increase in every other stitch—36 stitches around.

Round 6: Work even.

Round 7: Increase in every 3rd stitch—48 stitches around.

Round 8: Work even.

Round 9: Increase in every 4th stitch—60 stitches around.

Round 10: Work even.

Round 11: Increase in every 5th stitch—72 stitches around.

Round 12: Work even.

Round 13: Increase in every 6th stitch—84 stitches around.

Round 14: Work even.

Round 15: Increase in every 7th stitch—96 stitches around.

Round 16: Work even.

Round 17: Increase in every 8th stitch—108 stitches around.

Round 18: Work even.

Round 19: Increase in every 9th stitch—120 stitches around.

Round 20: Work even.

Round 21: Increase in every 20th stitch—126 stitches around.

Rounds 22 through 32: Work even. At the end of Round 32, begin joining rounds.

Round 33: Increase in every 25th stitch—131 stitches around.

Round 34: Work even.

Round 35: Increase in every 26th stitch—136 stitches around.

Round 36: Work even. Mold the top of the crown by pushing in the top of the dome, pushing the center back out, and denting the front edge slightly.

Round 37: Increase in every 27th stitch—141 stitches around.

Round 38: Work even.

Round 39: Increase in every 28th stitch—146 stitches around. Join and fasten off. Tie on yarn B.

Round 40: Work even. Fasten off and tie on yarn C.

Round 41: Increase in every 36th stitch—150 stitches around.

Round 42: Work even. Fasten off and tie on B.

Round 43: Work even. Fasten off and tie on C.

Rounds 44 and 45: Work even. At the end of Round 45, fasten off and tie on B.

Round 46: Work even. Fasten off and tie on C.

Rounds 47 and 48: Work even. At the end of Round 48, fasten off and tie on B.

Round 49: Work even. Fasten off and tie on C.

Rounds 50 and 51: Work even. Fasten off and tie on B.

Round 52: Work even. Fasten off.

BRIM:

Round 1: Tie on yarn A and, crocheting into only the outer loop of each stitch in the previous round, increase in every 12th stitch—162 stitches around.

Round 2: Working again into both loops of stitches in the previous round, increase in every 13th stitch—174 stitches around.

Round 3: Work even.

Round 4: Increase in every 14th stitch—186 stitches around.

Round 5: Work even.

Round 6: Increase in every 15th stitch—198 stitches around.

Round 7: Work even.

Round 8: Increase in every 16th stitch—210 stitches around.

Round 9: Work even.

Round 10: Increase in every 17th stitch—222 stitches around.

Round 11: Work even.

Round 12: Increase in every 18th stitch—234 stitches around.

Round 13: Work even.

Round 14: Increase in every 19th stitch—246 stitches around.

Round 15: Work even.

Round 16: Increase in every 20th stitch—258 stitches around. Begin joining rounds.

Round 17: Work even.

Hem facing is available in a wide range of colors, and stitched inside the hat crown, makes an ideal sweatband.

Round 18: Increase in every 21st stitch—270 stitches around.

Rounds 19 and 20: Work even. Join, fasten off, and carefully work in the fastened-off yarn end. Take the hem facing and sew it inside the hat as a sweatband.

To make this hat at a looser gauge of 5 stitches to the inch, work according to the following instructions:

CROWN:

Rounds 1 through 14: Work as previously instructed for the hat.

Round 15: Increase in every 10th stitch—92 stitches around.

Round 16: Work even.

Round 17: Increase in every 18th stitch—97 stitches around.

Rounds 18 through 25: Work even. Mold the top of the crown by pushing in the top of the dome, pushing out the center back, and denting the front edge slightly. At the end of Round 25, begin joining rounds.

Round 26: Increase in every 24th stitch—101 stitches around.

Round 27: Work even.

Round 28: Increase in every 25th stitch—105 stitches around.

Round 29: Work even.

Round 30: Increase in every 26th stitch—109 stitches around. Join and fasten off. Tie on yarn B.

Round 31: Work even. Fasten off and tie on C.

Round 32: Increase in every 36th stitch—112 stitches around.

Round 33: Work even. Fasten off and tie on B.

Round 34: Increase in every 37th stitch—115 stitches around. Fasten off and tie on C.

Rounds 35 and 36: Work even. At the end of Round 36, fasten off and tie on B.

Round 37: Work even. Fasten off and tie on C.

Rounds 38 and 39: Work even. At the end of Round 39, fasten off and tie on B.

Round 40: Work even. At the end of the round, fasten off.

BRIM:

Round 1: Tie on yarn A and, crocheting into only the outer loop of each stitch in the previous round, increase in every 10th stitch—127 stitches around.

Round 2: Working again into both loops of stitches in the previous round, increase in every 11th stitch—139 stitches around.

Round 3: Work even.

Round 4: Increase in every 12th stitch—151 stitches around.

Round 5: Work even.

Round 6: Increase in every 13th stitch—163 stitches around.

Round 7: Work even.

Round 8: Increase in every 14th stitch—175 stitches around.

Round 9: Work even.

Round 10: Increase in every 15th stitch—187 stitches around.

Round 11: Work even.

Round 12: Increase in every 16th stitch—199 stitches around.

Round 13: Work even.

Round 14: Increase in every 17th stitch—211 stitches around.

Round 15: Work even.

Round 16: Increase in every 18th stitch—223 stitches around.

Rounds 17 and 18: Work even. Join, fasten off, and carefully work in the fastened-off yarn end. Take the hem facing and sew it inside the hat as a sweatband.

HAT 2

The shape of this hat is more than a little reminiscent of the hats worn by Indians native to South America's high Andes. The horse-motif (or llama, if you prefer) pattern, unlike those worked in baskets, is worked from the top down; consequently, the design is penciled in with the pattern graph turned upside down. To work the design from the graph, it is necessary to turn the graph right-side up so the heads of the horses are pointing downward and their feet are sticking up in the air.

This hat is also unusual in that it is worked in the round and then superblocked on a hat block. Hat blocks are sold in millinery supply stores, and having one is worthwhile if you contemplate making this and similar hats.

Dimensions: Crown—5 inches high by 22 inches around the base (hat size: 7); brim—2 inches wide.

Yarn: Two colors of three-ply acrylic/modacrylic carpet yarn or a suitable substitute—approximately 5 ounces of the darker yarn and 3 ounces of the lighter.

Hook: Steel #1.

Gauge: 6.5 stitches = 1 inch.

Hat 2

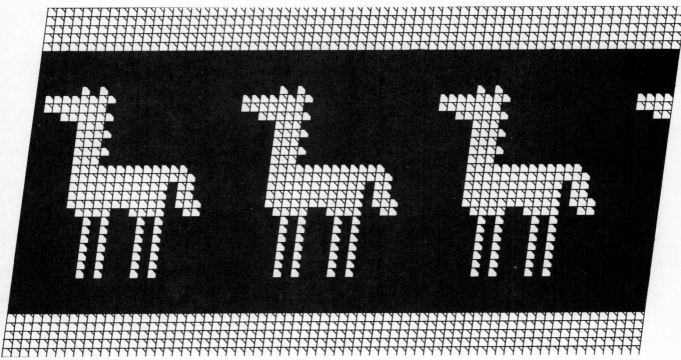

Design graph, Hat 2

CROWN:

With the darker yarn, chain 4 and connect the ends of the chain with a Slip Stitch.

Rounds 1 through 3: Increase in each stitch around until there are 24 stitches around.

Round 4: Work even. Begin joining rounds.

Round 5: Increase in every other stitch—36 stitches around.

Round 6: Work even.

Round 7: Increase in every 3rd stitch—48 stitches around.

Round 8: Work even.

Round 9: Increase in every 4th stitch—60 stitches around.

Round 10: Work even.

Round 11: Increase in every 5th stitch—72 stitches around.

Round 12: Work even.

Round 13: Increase in every 6th stitch—84 stitches around.

Round 14: Work even.

Round 15: Increase in every 7th stitch—96 stitches around.

Round 16: Work even.

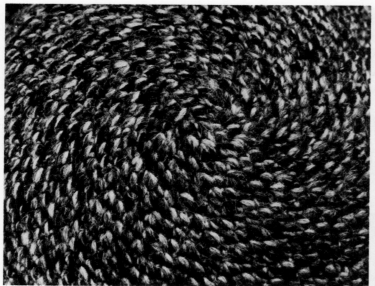

It's almost impossible to make out the individual stitches in the hat's superblocked crown.

A closer look at one of the hat's five horses (or llamas).

Round 17: Increase in every 8th stitch—108 stitches around.

Round 18: Work even. Lightly block the shape on the hat block.

Round 19: Increase in every 12th stitch—117 stitches around.

Round 20: Work even.

Round 21: Increase in every 15th stitch—125 stitches around. Begin carrying the lighter yarn.

Round 22: Work even. Begin following the design graph, allowing 22 stitches between each of the five design elements in the first design round.

Round 23: Work 5 increases, one between each horse —130 stitches around.

Round 24: Work even.

Round 25: Increase once between each horse—135 stitches around.

Round 26: Work even.

Round 27: Increase once between each horse—140 stitches around.

Round 28: Work even.

Round 29: Increase once between each horse—145 stitches around.

Round 30: Work even.

Round 31: Increase once between each horse—150 stitches around.

Rounds 32 through 43: Work even. Superblock the finished crown.

BRIM:

Stop carrying the lighter-colored yarn just before joining the last round in the crown.

Round 1: Working into the outside loops of the bottom round of the crown, increase in every 15th stitch around—160 stitches around. Continue joining rounds.

Round 2: Work even. Work again into both loops in the previous round.

Round 3: Increase in every 16th stitch—170 stitches around.

Round 4: Work even.

Round 5: Increase in every 17th stitch—180 stitches around.

Round 6: Work even.

Round 7: Increase in every 18th stitch—190 stitches around.

Round 8: Work even.

Round 9: Increase in every 19th stitch—200 stitches around.

Rounds 10 and 11: Work even. Join, fasten off, and carefully work in the fastened-off yarn end.

Superblock the brim.

HAT 3

Working a flat round out and down isn't the only way to make a hat crown—the same dome shape can be had by crocheting individual wedgelike segments and joining them together. The hat shown here consists of eight identical segments, each terminating in a 45-degree angle

Hat 3

point. When joined, the eight points come together (Fig. 131) to form the 360-degree top of the crown.

A shiny brass grommet is set into each superblocked segment; the joined segments are reblocked on a dome-shaped hat block; a multicolored brim is worked out from the bottom of the crown. Sewing a colorful sweatband inside completes this unusual hat.

FIGURE 131

Dimensions: Crown—4 inches high by 22 inches around at the base (hat size: 7); brim—2 inches wide.

Yarn: Eight different colors of three-ply acrylic/mod-acrylic carpet yarn or suitable substitutes—small quantities each of a black or dark gray, a light gray, and six other colors.

Hooks: Steel #0 for the crown; steel #1 for the brim.

Gauges: 5.5 stitches = 1 inch for the crown; 6.5 stitches = 1 inch for the brim.

Additional Materials: Little brass grommets and a grommet setter.

CROWN:

With any one of the eight colors, chain 13.

Row 1: Work a row of Singles back over the chain, working into the back of the chain for a finished chain edge —12 stitches across.

Rows 2 through 13: Work even.

Row 14: Decrease once in the middle of the row—11 stitches across.

Row 15: Work even.

Row 16: Decrease once in the middle of the row—10 stitches across.

Row 17: Work even.

Row 18: Decrease once in the middle of the row—9 stitches across.

Row 19: Work even. In the middle of the row, chain 1 and skip the middle (5th) stitch.

Row 20: Work even. Work a Single into the chain in the middle of the previous row.

Row 21: Decrease once in the middle of the row—8 stitches across.

Using a simple grommet setter, grommets are fixed into each of the hat's segments.

Row 22: Work even.

Row 23: Decrease once in the middle of the row—7 stitches across.

Row 24: Work even.

Row 25: Decrease once in the middle of the row—6 stitches across.

Row 26: Decrease twice, at the beginning of the row and at the end of the row—4 stitches across.

Row 27: Work even.

Row 28: Decrease once at the end of the row—3 stitches across.

Row 29: Decrease once at the end of the row—2 stitches across.

Row 30: Decrease once—1 stitch across.

Row 31: Work a Single into the Single in the previous "row."

Fasten off.

Make seven more segments like the one above with the seven remaining colors.

Border the three lightest-colored segments and the light gray segment with the black or dark gray yarn, darker segments and the dark gray or black segment with the light gray yarn. Double increase around points and bottom corners; increase in every 6th stitch along the raw edges.

Using the grommet setter, set a grommet into each hole left between Rows 19 and 20 of each segment.

Superblock each segment, and then decide how you want the colors arranged in the finished hat. At first stitch the segments together in pairs with their fronts facing; stitch into only the outside loops of the joined edges. When you have four pairs of joined segments, join the pairs to complete the dome shape. Block the finished crown on the hat block.

The points will not meet, and a quarter-sized space will remain at the top of the crown. Crochet a small flat round and stitch it in to plug up the hole.

Crocheting with one while carrying the other, use the dark gray or black yarn and the light gray yarn to work around the bottom of the crown—crochet dark stitches over dark and light over light. Increase in the round, alternating between an increase in every 4th stitch and every 5th stitch. There should be 136 stitches in the completed round.

Stitched to the points of the joined segments, a quarter-sized flat round fills the gap that remains at the top of the crown.

138

BRIM:

Tie one of the six segment colors to the last round.

Round 1: Crocheting into only the outside loops and carrying a length of the yarn being crocheted, alternate between increasing in every 5th stitch and every 6th stitch—160 stitches around. Begin joining rounds.

Round 2: Crocheting into both loops in the previous round, increase in every 20th stitch—168 stitches around. At the beginning of the round, clip the carried yarn and begin carrying one of the other segment colors.

Round 3: At the join, bring up the carried color and begin crocheting with it while carrying the other color. Work even.

Round 4: Increase in every 21st stitch—176 stitches around. At the beginning of the round, clip the carried yarn and begin carrying a different segment color.

Round 5: At the join, bring up the carried yarn and begin crocheting with it while carrying the other color. Work even.

Round 6: Increase in every 22nd stitch—184 stitches around. At the beginning of the round, clip the carried yarn and begin carrying one of the other segment colors.

Round 7: At the join, bring up the carried yarn and begin crocheting with it while carrying the other color. Work even.

Round 8: Increase in every 23rd stitch—192 stitches around. At the beginning of the round, clip the carried yarn and begin carrying a new segment color.

Round 9: At the join, bring up the new color and begin crocheting with it while carrying the other yarn. Work even.

Round 10: Increase in every 24th stitch—200 stitches around. At the beginning of the round, clip the carried yarn and begin carrying either the dark gray or black yarn or the light gray yarn, depending on the color being worked.

Round 11: At the join, bring up the carried yarn and begin crocheting with it while carrying the other color. Work even. Join, fasten off, and work in the fastened-off yarn end. Block the brim.

Attaché Case

This is definitely not the first thing to attempt in Hard Crochet. Make a number of other objects first, fool around with designing and executing some things on your own, get real good at crocheting hard with a hook with a homemade handle, cancel any long-term plans, get plenty of rest and drink liquids, *then* try making this attaché case.

Crocheting this attaché isn't quite as difficult as I've made it out to be, but it is a pretty ambitious project, one that demands great accuracy, a high degree of hook control, and a willingness to rip out stitches more than just a few times. To put it in more positive terms, constructing this attaché case is a genuine challenge; if you feel up to it, give it a go. If you succeed, the reward will not be something you carry around casually.

Dimensions: 14½ inches long by 10 inches high by 2 inches wide.

Yarn: Four colors of three-ply acrylic/modacrylic carpet yarn or suitable substitutes—approximately 20 ounces of yarn A and small quantities of yarns B, C, and D.

Hook: Steel #1.

Gauge: 6 inches = 1 inch.

Additional Materials: One 15-inch-long, heavy-duty zipper; two 9-inch-long, ¼-inch-diameter aluminum rods.

SIDE PANELS (2):

With yarn A, make a Slip Knot with a very long yarn end—about 8 yards long (roll the long end into a ball to prevent tangling). Chain 61.

Row 1: Work Singles back over the chain, working into the back of the chain for a finished chain edge—60 stitches across.

Row 2: Begin carrying the long Slip Knot end. Increase at the beginning and end of the row—62 stitches across.

Rows 3 through 26: Work even. In the middle of Row 26, stop carrying yarn A and begin carrying yarn B.

Row 27: Bring up yarn B and begin crocheting with it while carrying yarn A. In the middle of the row, stop carrying A and begin carrying yarn C.

Rows 28, 29, and 30: Bring up C and begin carrying B. Work 3 rows with C.

Row 31: Bring up B and carry C. In the middle of the row, stop carrying C and start carrying yarn D.

Rows 32, 33, and 34: Bring up D and begin carrying B. Work D for 3 rows.

Row 35: Bring up B and carry D to the middle of the row; there, stop carrying D and begin carrying C.

Rows 36, 37, and 38: Bring up C and carry B for 3 rows.

Row 39: Bring up B and carry C to the middle of the row; there, stop carrying C and start carrying D.

Rows 40, 41, and 42: Bring up D and carry B for 3 rows.

Row 43: Bring up B and carry D to the middle of the row; there, stop carrying D and begin carrying C.

Rows 44, 45, and 46: Bring up C and carry B for 3 rows.

Row 47: Bring up B and carry C to the middle of the row; there, stop carrying C and start carrying yarn A again.

Rows 48 through 72: Bring up A and carry B to the middle of Row 48; there, stop carrying B and begin carrying a long—8 yards, again—strand of A.

Row 73: Decrease at the beginning and at the end of the row.

Row 74: Work even. At the end of the row, fasten off and clip the remaining length of carried yarn.

With yarn A, work a bordering row of Single Crochet around the entire panel, increasing in every 6th stitch space along the raw-edge sides of the panel. Do not, however, border the stripe design with yarn A. Instead, 10 stitches or so from the design, begin carrying a strand of yarn B; bring up B to work only across the design; bring up A and continue the border, dropping B after 10 or so stitches.

Make another panel exactly like the first. With a hot iron and a wet covering cloth, superblock both panels.

GUSSET:

With yarn A, make a Slip Knot with a very long yarn end—about 10 yards long. Chain 11.

Row 1: Work Singles back over the chain, working into the back of the chain for a finished chain edge—10 stitches across.

Rows 2 through 170: Carrying the long yarn end, work even rows until the gusset section is 170 rows long. Fasten off and clip the remaining length of carried yarn.

Border around the gusset with yarn A, increasing in every 6th space along the sides. Superblock.

HANDLES (2):

Note: the handles are crocheted slightly tighter (6.5 stitches to the inch) than the other sections.

With yarn A, make a Slip Knot with a long yarn end—about 3 feet long—and chain 10.

Row 1: Work Singles back over the chain, working into the back of the chain for a finished chain edge—9 stitches across.

Rows 2 through 27: Carrying the long Slip Knot end, work even.

Row 28: Work the 9 stitches in the row as follows: 3 Singles; 3 Half Doubles; 3 Doubles.

Row 29: Work 9 Singles.

Row 30: Work the same as Row 28.

Row 31: Return to crocheting only Singles. At the end of the row, stop carrying yarn A.

Row 32: Start carrying yarn B from the beginning of the row.

Rows 33 through 53: Work the B–C–B–D–B–C–B–D–B–C–B stripe design.

Row 54: Bring up yarn A and carry B to the end of the row; there, stop carrying B.

Row 55: Begin carrying a long strand of yarn A.

Row 56: Work 3 Singles, 3 Half Doubles, and 3 Doubles.

Row 57: Work Singles.

Row 58: Work 3 Singles, 3 Half Doubles, and 3 Doubles.

Rows 59 through 85: Work even rows of Singles to the end of Row 85 and fasten off.

Border the handle piece with yarn A, working across the stripe design with yarn B. Increase in every 6th space along the sides, but add an additional increase along each of the shapes outside curves (see Fig. 132), and eliminate one increase along each of the shapes inside curves (see Fig. 133).

Make a second handle piece exactly like the first and superblock both.

Take the two aluminum rods and, with a pair of pliers, bend each of them into the shape shown in Figure 134. The distance between the two parallel ends should be 5½ inches. Thread two blunt-nosed needles, one with a length of yarn A (1 foot will do) and the other with a similar length of yarn B. Wrap the handle piece around the rod (right side facing out) and stitch the sides together. Stitch the middle design area's edges together first with yarn B. Stitch the edges together on both sides of the design with yarn A, leaving 2½ inches at each end unstitched, as in Figure 135. The completed handle should look like Figure 136.

ZIPPER:

With yarn A, chain 101. Working into the back of the chain for a finished chain edge, work a row of Singles back over the chain—100 stitches across.

Row 2: Work even.

Row 3: Work even and fasten off.

Make another long, narrow strip like the first. Superblock both.

Holding the two long strips parallel to each other and with their respective finished chain edges facing each

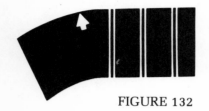

FIGURE 132

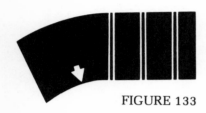

FIGURE 133

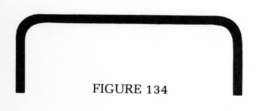

FIGURE 134

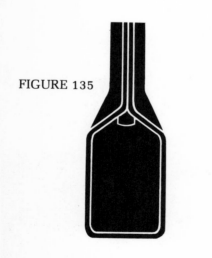

FIGURE 135

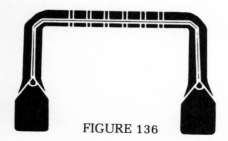

FIGURE 136

other, "join" the ends of the two strips in the manner shown in Figure 137 (the dots represent Singles and the dashes represent chains). Turn and work back over the first three Singles, into the three chains, and in the last three Singles—9 stitches across. In the next row, decrease at both ends of the row—7 stitches across. Decrease at both ends of the next row—5 stitches across. Work a final row with a decrease in the middle of the row—4 stitches across. Fasten off and superblock the entire piece.

With the bottom end of the zipper (the end the glide is at when the zipper is open) at the end where the two strips are joined, sew the zipper to the undersides of the strips, allowing enough room on either side for the glide to slide easily between the strips (Fig. 138).

FIGURE 137

FIGURE 138

Count the bordering stitches all along the long side of the gusset. Then count the bordering stitches along the two short sides and the long bottom side of the side panels. You should count a few more stitches in the side panels. Evenly distribute this difference when you begin stitching the gusset to the side panel.

Lacing back and forth with a threaded strand of yarn A, attach the gusset to the side panels, one side panel at a time. Stitch through both loops in both edges. Stitch the gusset to the stripe design at the bottom of the panel with yarn B.

Sew the zipper to the top edges of the side panels with yarn A, using yarn B to stitch the design area. Allow the closed-off end of the zipper to flop beyond the end of the case.

Attach the handles to the case by stitching right through the open end of the handle and the side of the case, as in Figure 139 (the little dots indicate the places where stitches are made). With both handles attached, the attaché case is complete.

FIGURE 139

Puppets

The two puppets shown here are related—they're brothers, and they live together in the private collection of jewelry designer Rhodia Mann. The longer-nosed of the two (a nose which, by the way, is crocheted around a real, honkable bicycle horn) goes by the name of Harpo; the bespectacled fellow is, of course, his brother Groucho. To give any puppet the rigidness of these two, all you have to do is say the secret words: Hard Crochet.

Groucho, detail.

146

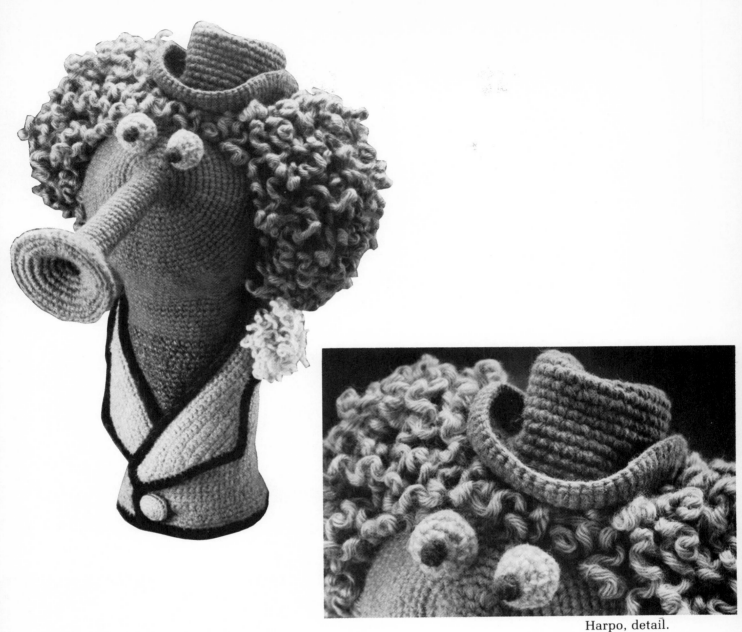

Harpo, detail.

There isn't enough space here to explain how each of these puppets was made, which is as it should be. Puppets are fun things and fun to make, and half the fun of making them is figuring out how simple elements—domes, tubes, small back-and-forth shapes—can be put together so they come to life. The hair on both Harpo and Groucho, however, deserves explaining. Yarn was crocheted into a tight, square swatch; the swatch was superblocked; the yarn was ripped out and snipped into short, kinky strands that were then individually attached to the puppets' heads.

SUPPLIERS OF YARNS FOR HARD CROCHET

The Mannings Creative Crafts
R.D. 2
East Berlin, Pennsylvania 17316

If it wasn't for The Mannings and their yarn, there might not be a Hard Crochet today. Here is the only source I know of for the three-ply acrylic/modacrylic carpet yarns. For fifty cents, The Mannings will send samples of their current stock of these yarns. Just ask for the yarns for Hard Crochet, and The Mannings will know what you want.

The Mannings ask only that you order at least a pound of each color (there are approximately five hundred yards in a pound of three-ply carpet yarn) and that orders be for no less than five pounds. The yarn comes on cones, but you do not pay for the weight of the cone.

The Mannings always assume you're in a terrific hurry to get your yarn—the day they receive your order is the day they send out the yarn. I once put an order in the mail on a Monday and received my yarn (via UPS) on the following Friday.

The Weaver's Store
36 Boylston Street
(in The Garage)
Cambridge, Massachusetts 02138

Both the basket with the incredible weight-lifting ability on page 18 and the basket with the Yurok Indian design on page 96 were made with yarn from The Weaver's Store, where one never knows for sure what one is going to find in the way of unusual synthetic yarns.

I have arranged with Phyllis Damon, The Weaver's Store's indefatigable whirlwind of a founder, to try out new yarns as they become available to see which ones are best suited to Hard Crochet. Send fifty cents and you'll get back samples of these and lots of others. And information concerning the very liberal conditions for ordering yarns by mail will be included with requested samples.

If you are in the Boston area and would like to visit, go to The Garage at 36 Boylston Street in Cambridge.

The two suppliers listed are not the only mill-end dealers around. If you look under "Yarn" in your Yellow Pages, you just might find some people who have yarns that crochet up very hard. And do visit shops in your area that cater to weavers and serious fiber artists; don't forget to take a couple of hooks with homemade handles along to try anything you might find. Having to search out materials is one of the adventures that goes along with practicing a new craft technique.